# AMERICA'S SUPER HORSE
## *The Story of Rugged Lark*

COPYRIGHT ©2000 REBEKAH F. WITTER

RUGGED LARK NAME COPYRIGHT ©2000 CAROL A. HARRIS

JACKET DESIGN BY ENDEAVOR GRAPHICS, A DIVISION OF ENDEAVOR PUBLICATIONS, INC.
INTERNAL DESIGN BY ENDEAVOR GRAPHICS, A DIVISION OF ENDEAVOR PUBLICATIONS, INC.

FRONT COVER PASTEL BY DEBBIE FITZGERALD
BACK COVER PHOTOGRAPH BY LESLIE GROVES, THE QUARTER HORSE JOURNAL
AUTHOR PHOTO ©2000 REBEKAH F. WITTER

PHOTO CREDITS AND COPYRIGHTS AT BACK

All rights reserved. No part of this book may be reproduced in any form or by any electronic or mechanical means including information storage and retrieval systems–except in the case of brief quotations embodied in critical articles or reviews–without permission from its publisher, Endeavor Publications, Inc. except where permitted by law.

LIBRARY OF CONGRESS CATALOGING-IN-PUBLICATION DATA IS ON FILE WITH THE PUBLISHER.

ISBN 0-9704110-0-6

PUBLISHED BY
ENDEAVOR PUBLICATIONS, INC.
OCALA ~ RALEIGH ~ FORT LAUDERDALE
3622 N.E. JACKSONVILLE RD. ~ OCALA, FLORIDA 34479
352-369-1104
FAX: 352-369-1108
PRINTED AND BOUND IN THE UNITED STATES OF AMERICA

October, 2000

To Nancy and Greg — both
I'm so glad you love
love horses 'cause I love
people who love horses, and also
I'm glad that you are going
to read my story, I hope
you enjoy it and always
remember that I'm your friend
Love from
Rugged Lark + Carol
2000

©Cappy Jackson

To Mike,

I would like to dedicate this story to you in hopes that you can put your Columbus, Ohio nightmare to rest. I am totally convinced that you had nothing to do with Lark's overspin at the 1984 Congress Reining Futurity. Your pilot error was simply part of Rugged Lark's destiny...and without it we might never have discovered his many talents.

*Carol*

# Table of Contents

| | | |
|---|---|---|
| Introduction | | viiii |
| Foreword by Bill Brewer | | xiii |
| Chapter 1 | Golden Heritage<br>"Star Crossing" | 1 |
| Chapter 2 | Field of Diamonds<br>"Calling All Studs!" | 16 |
| Chapter 3 | Spinning to Destiny<br>"The Launch and a Flameout" | 23 |
| Chapter 4 | The Hunt for Plan B<br>"Get Right Back On..." | 35 |
| Chapter 5 | A Matter of Trust...and Love<br>"Championship Philosophy" | 43 |
| Chapter 6 | In the Palm of Her Hand<br>"Winning Team Formula" | 55 |
| Chapter 7 | Six-Year-Old Retiree<br>"Retired and Still Winning" | 77 |
| Chapter 8 | One Moment in Time<br>"From Superhorse to Super Star" | 89 |
| Chapter 9 | Horse Play<br>"Who's in the Horse Suit?" | 109 |
| Chapter 10 | Fan Fare<br>"Caramel Corn and Champagne" | 135 |
| Chapter 11 | An Exaltation of Larks<br>"Superhorse Legacy" | 155 |
| Postscript | Carol Has the Last Word | 179 |
| Author's Note | | 187 |
| Acknowledgements | | 191 |

# Introduction
## "Karmic Ribbons"

One of life's fascinations is found in serendipity, kismet, fate, providence.... All those curious karmic ribbons that bind us together—one to another—creating the texture of our destinies.

In March of 1999, a family wedding brought me from northern California to Ocala, Florida. Release of a new book brought me an invitation from Barnes and Noble for an author-talk and book-signing. Arriving early, I found to my amazed delight that my book event was headline news in Ocala's Star Banner. As the newly proclaimed "Horse Capital of the United States", any- and everything horse-related in Ocala's Marion County is newsworthy.

After checking into my room, I happened upon an ad for a local equestrian gallery and took down the address to visit—if time allowed. Late that afternoon, I found The Paddock Room, a showplace for equestrian art, accessories and gifts. When I walked in, the owner was "talking horse" with another woman and I interjected a quip about "living on horse time" that struck a congenial chord. The other woman stared quizzically, saying I looked familiar, but.... When I introduced myself, she realized. "You're the woman in the paper who's speaking tomorrow! I wanted to go, but I've got a dinner engagement. The topic is close to my heart because my horses teach me new life lessons everyday." Gesturing, she said, "Come with me; I'd like to show you my horse."

Following her into the adjoining room, I saw a large portrait of a stunning bay Quarter Horse. The recognition was instantaneous and I exclaimed, "That's your horse? You own Rugged Lark?"

The woman nodded, smiling, "Yes, I'm Carol Harris."

"Oh, wow," I gushed, suddenly sounding like a star-struck teenager. "I've followed his career for years...I'm a regular Rugged Lark groupie!"

"In that case—if you have time—why don't you stop by and meet him?"

I couldn't believe my luck! Rock stars hold little interest for me, but horse stars, now that's a different story—this was way up on my thrill list.

"My husband's flying in tonight...could he come, too?" I asked hesitantly.

"Sure, bring him along."

So, while the wedding party was busy rehearsing, Kip and I went off to meet a horse...and fell in love.

When we arrived at Bo-Bett Farm, Rugged Lark had just been brought back from the breeder's. Under such circumstances, I'd expected a stallion would still be high, but Lark sauntered over casually when Carol let us into his paddock. Carol greeted him and introduced us, "Lark, I'd like you to meet Mr. and Mrs. Witter" Politely, the stallion curtsied. Well, that was it. Our hearts melted.

Then Carol asked if he was being a good boy. He nodded affirmatively. When she asked, "Are you ever a bad boy, Lark?" he emphatically shook his head, "No, never, not me." We were charmed.

After a short photo shoot, our visit with Lark ended with Carol explaining that we had to head back to California. With that, Lark stretched down in a gallant bow of farewell. We were hooked.

Carol then invited us in to her office to view a video collage of some of Lark's most memorable performances. We were touched and awed.

As we left, Carol mentioned that she was planning a book on Rugged Lark and I said, "Put me down for a copy—that's one biography I want to read!"

Carol said, "Actually, I think you're the very person to write it."

So with that serendipitous wedding trip, that chance? meeting at The Paddock Room, I met Carol Harris and got to write the book on Rugged Lark. Much of Carol's and Rugged Lark's story shines with their very own colorful karmic ribbons—the twist of genetic fate that produced this singular stallion; the death and the dream that led Carol to buy him; the devastating competition that providentially opened new arenas; the unusual training that became his hallmark; the Olympic theme that became his signature...the lifelong legend that continues to grow with his talented get. These stories will excite, inspire, charm and touch you, as you, too, fall under the spell of Carol Harris and her beloved Rugged Lark—America's Super Horse.

©Cappy Jackson

Bill Brewer

Executive Vice President

American Quarter Horse Association

# Foreward

## by Bill Brewer

Nearly every sports discipline has its heroes. From the Mantle's to the McGwire's and from the Bradshaw's to the Elway's, they have all left an indelible mark on the sports they played. Thankfully, the American Quarter Horse industry has had its fair share of superstars, and I believe no discussion about those athletes would be complete without spending time on Rugged Lark.

I first saw Rugged Lark in 1985 at the All-American Quarter Horse Congress. During the show, Lynn Palm was riding him. Because I had known Carol Harris for many years, I was particularly interested in her horses. I remember Lark having that special look that so many American Quarter Horses possess - it's one you notice immediately in their eyes.

The following month, I had the privilege of watching Rugged Lark and Lynn compete at the AQHA World Championship Show and the more I watched him, the more I liked him. He moved with such willingness and presence, and I loved his head. You could tell he had a great attitude. Obviously, the judges also saw this in him because he won his first Superhorse title that year.

I believed in Rugged Lark's honesty because he competed in both English and Western events, which truly exemplified what I considered a World Show Superhorse. Of course, when he won his second Superhorse crown in 1987, I was even more impressed.

For those of us who really love horses, it's easy to understand that Rugged Lark's big, kind eye, intelligent expression and gentle disposition are reasons why so many people throughout the world love American Quarter Horses.

Rugged Lark has been an extraordinary goodwill ambassador for AQHA and the American Quarter Horse breed because of his willingness, versatility, gentleness and balance. He has all that, and he has proven his ability to pass those most desirable traits along to his offspring. The fact that Rugged Lark also has sired two other World Show Superhorses–1991's "The Lark Ascending" and 1999's "Look Who's Larkin' "–is further evidence of his ability. A glance at Rugged Lark's AQHA sire record should give all of us comfort in realizing that his name will be included in any discussion about outstanding sires.

Rugged Lark has helped AQHA, as much as any human has, to achieve our quest to have Reining become an Olympic event. In 1989, at the World Cup competition in Tampa, Florida, Rugged Lark performed for the first time to "One Moment In Time". I've seen that performance several times since then and it always brings a tear to my eye.

Whether it was in Florida, Oklahoma, Georgia or New Jersey, no matter where Rugged Lark made his appearances, he was always overwhelmed by hundreds of cute little girls who were clamoring to touch him. You know, you could tell he loved it. In fact, I think he was flirting with them because he wanted them to pet him so badly.

My most sincere thanks to Carol for documenting Rugged Lark's career and to Lark for all your contributions and for being an AQHA hero to so many people.

Bill Brewer
American Quarter Horse Association
Executive Vice President

# AMERICA'S SUPER HORSE

## *The Story of Rugged Lark*

By

Rebekah F. Witter

*An oil painting by Bob Judy depicting Rugged Lark enjoying a bath.*

# Chapter One
# Golden Heritage
## "Star Crossing"

"Oh, he's gorgeous!" Carol Harris exclaimed to her husband, Buck, as her new Thoroughbred, Really Rugged, was unloaded from the horse van. The brilliant Florida sun rippled like liquid mercury along the stallion's muscular back as he was led quietly around the parking area in front of Bo-Bett Farm's show barn. His rich mahogany coat, silky black mane and tail, and elegant ebony legs stood out in dramatic contrast against the bright white limestone driveway.

"Well, you asked Joe to find you a horse with good looks and good legs," said Buck. "He says Really Rugged is 'one of the best-looking S.O.B.'s that ever raced.'"

Out of the Florida Hall of Fame mare, Ruddy Belle, Really Rugged was sired by renowned Thoroughbred breeder, Joe O'Farrell's all-time favorite stud, Rough'n Tumble. "Rough", as Joe called him, was a famous foundation sire for the Florida racing industry. He'd sired a slew of winners in the 1950's including Dr. Fager and My Dear Girl, earning more than $4 million...when $4 million was considered real money.

"With just three wins, three seconds and five thirds, Really Rugged never really hit his stride at the track. Joe said he only earned about seventeen grand, but he had an excuse, an accident stopped him cold," Carol added. "But his conformation's great and I think he's just what we need to add some speed to my Quarter Horse racing bloodlines."

*(top photo) Really Rugged - Sire of Rugged Lark*

*(bottom photo) Buck Harris*

"Really Big" a son of Really Rugged, who won countless distance races at Pompano Park, Florida. He was owned by Carol Harris & Doc & Evonne Severinson of The Tonight Show fame.

A fan of this horse told Carol one night that he "thought Really Big was the best horse in the whole world because every stick of furniture in his house was bought & paid for by his winning tickets on "Really Big". On this night, he finished the kitchen.

Suddenly, a worker came running, calling, "Mr. Harris! Come quick! One of the calves is drowning!"

Buck looked over to the distant pond and saw a cow with a tiny calf struggling to keep its nose above water. In one smooth arc, he grabbed the saddle he was returning to the barn, swung it onto the young stallion's back, secured the cinch, untied the rope, grabbed the lead-line from the startled groom and took off!

Since the pasture gate had been left open, they raced full-tilt to the pond, never slowing until they splashed in, chest-deep to the drowning animal's side. Buck dropped his loop over the calf's head and dragged it safely ashore.

"That's a helluva test for a young stud," remarked Buck as he and Carol walked Really Rugged back to the barn. "I'm sure glad he took it all so well.... Maybe his racing problem was that he's really a ropin' horse at heart."

Stroking the stallion's wet neck, Buck chuckled, "Yup, you're one helluva Thoroughbred cow-pony!"

Lured by the sun and an extended training season, Carol Harris had moved her active Quarter Horse breeding operation in the early 1960's from northern New Jersey to Reddick, Florida. The area's vast, rolling pastures boast a limestone-rich soil that fortifies the grass and strengthens equine bones. This environmental anomaly had been attracting Thoroughbred breeders for decades, but Carol was among the first Quarter Horse enthusiasts to move into the area around Ocala, Florida. A savvy breeder who understands the value of hybrid vigor, Carol found herself surrounded by some of the best race horses in the country. Since Thoroughbreds are the only official outcross sanctioned by the American Quarter Horse Association (AQHA), Carol quickly decided to use the speedy local Thoroughbreds to bolster her Quarter Horse racing program.

The 1964 purchase of Really Rugged not only provided the desired speed, this remarkable stallion also passed on his classic conformation, incredibly quick mind and exceptionally calm demeanor. Really Rugged enjoyed a happy, healthy life at Bo-Bett Farm siring many beautiful and successful competitors on the Quarter Horse racing circuit and in the show ring. Among Carol's favorites were Mr. Doin' Good, Rugged Punch, Really Sweet, Really Cool, Really Gone and Really Big.

When the first crop of Really Rugged foals went into training in 1968, it was apparent that something very different was at work here. Accustomed as they were to hot, anxious colts wired as tight as a Steinway piano, the exercise boys soon began joking about Really Rugged's offspring, "She thinks she's going to make runners out of these lazy babies?" The gentle, easy-going two-year-old's that Really Rugged sired seemed too laid-back to be serious contenders at anything involving speed.

It wasn't long before that joke turned around, however, for once the Bo-Bett youngsters got the hang of running, they put their strong hearts and eager minds into it: they raced calm, cool, and collected the winnings.

At Pompano Park, an appreciative racing fan who'd

*"Really Cool" sets a track record at Pompano Park, Florida on July 6, 1972.*

shared in some of those winnings told Carol, "Really Big's the best horse in the whole world—every stick of furniture in my house was bought and paid for by my win tickets on that horse."

In setting forth her breeding program, Carol Harris relies on both intellect and instinct. At times, she can't really pinpoint what leads her to a breeding decision, but she evidently saw some element in Really Rugged that she thought would spice up the reining arena, "I don't even know why I ever bred Really Rugged to Miss Lookin' Good," admits Carol. "She was a reining mare, but something made me do it and the result was Mr. Doin' Good, a big thoroughbred-y kind of a horse."

"He never looked like a reining horse—more like a hunt-seater—but he was a big-stopper, deadly leaded and could turn around with the best. For years he won for me and a number of other owners, earning top honors and a prominent spot in the Reining Horse Hall of Fame."

Some of Really Rugged's colts were simply too good-looking to be sent to the track—these were destined to compete as halter and performance horses. Rugged Punch was one that had been bred to race, but was redirected to the show ring and won the 1976 Pleasure Horse Futurity at the Quarter Horse Congress with Clark Bradley in the saddle.

Two years later Rugged Punch was being prepared for a return to the Congress in October, when late one August afternoon a thunderstorm

*(top photo) 2-year-olds in training at Bo-Bett Farm.*

*(bottom photo) Mr. Doin Good, with Bob Anthony aboard, the 1979 World Champion Open Reining Horse graces the cover of the NRHA Reiner.*

*Rugged Punch, with Clark Bradley, winning the 3-year-old Western Pleasure Futurity in 1976 at the All American Quarter Horse Congress. Breeder, Carol Harris, is to the left and owner, Wendy Winans, is pictured right accepting the award.*

blew over Bo-Bett. Several hours later, Carol's daughter, Wendy, found Rugged Punch on the ground outside the gate to his paddock. She called her mother over urgently—the metal gate was hanging off its hinges, and the horse was down and having trouble breathing.

In the dim light of the storm, neither could determine the problem, but Carol remembered noticing Rugged Punch well and happy in his paddock when she'd driven in earlier. Now, as she searched for the reason for his sudden, dire condition, Carol examined his swollen head and wondered if he might have been bitten by a snake?

With Wendy and Carol's encouragement and obvious effort, the stricken animal was finally able to scramble up. On wobbly legs, they led him, staggering like a newborn foal into the nearest stall. Out of the wind and in the light of the barn, the problem was revealed—the colt's forelock and eyelashes were singed and the acrid smell of burned hair stung Carol's nostrils. As she removed his halter, Carol saw to

her horror that the metal fittings had branded his cheeks and chin! Rugged Punch must have been standing by the metal gate when Mother Nature delivered her own really rugged punch—the force of a lightning strike had knocked the horse through the metal gate and welded his halter to his hide!

After examining him, the vet realized that Rugged Punch could no longer swallow, so he had to be tubed regularly with pellets dissolved in water to keep him going. Gradually, after about two weeks, his ability to swallow returned and he was strong enough to start back to work.

With Rugged Punch finally back under saddle, Wendy discovered the worst—the trauma had wiped the colt's memory clean. He'd forgotten all his training and didn't respond to the simplest of cues—no leads, no back-up, no nothin'. With the Congress now less than six weeks away, they were faced with having to re-educate Wendy's talented futurity champion from the very beginning.

Thankfully, in spite of his amnesia, Punch's mind was still willing. Less than two months after being struck by lightning, Wendy and Rugged Punch won the huge Amateur Pleasure Class at the All American Quarter Horse Congress. This resilient young horse with the prophetic name then went on to become a top working hunter, proving that despite having been hit with a truly rugged punch, he was not to be counted out.

Even though Really Rugged was producing such quick, kind, talented foals, he was still an undervalued gem at Bo-Bett Farm. Carol's first love and allegiance remained with her Quarter Horse stallions, Majestic Dell and Eternal Dell. In her mind they were the crown jewels of the Bo-Bett breeding program. Thoroughbreds such as Really Rugged only entered the mix to enhance her racing Quarter Horse interests.

On one visit, Carol's good friend, Mann Bailey, a successful cutting-horse rider, brought a highly respected rancher from

*(top photo) Rugged Punch and Wendy Winans on their way to winning the Amateur Western Pleasure at the 1978 All American Quarter Horse Congress.*

*(bottom photo) Rugged Punch and Molly Ebelhare in a winning ride in Working Hunter at the Florida Gold Coast Circuit.*

(top photo) Eternal Dell -
sired by Eternal Sun and out of Judy Dell by Poco Dell

(bottom photo) Mann Bailey on Rooster Clegg, his top cutting horse.

Arizona to Bo-Bett. The horseman toured the farm with sharp interest, appraising each animal silently with an expert eye. Afterwards, the group retired to the cool of the porch for drinks and horse talk. Carol was bursting with pride and curiosity as to how her beautiful horses measured up in the mind of this knowledgeable visitor.

They talked about this one and that one, and finally Buck asked, "Which one of the studs did you like the best?"

Carol just knew he would say "Eternal Dell" because he was such a handsome, modern horse with a gorgeous head and neck that possessed more natural elegance than most any other Quarter Horse, yet had the muscular hind legs so favored in the breed.

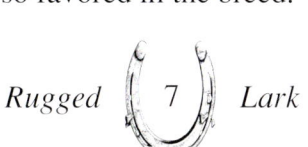

Rugged 7 Lark

The rancher pondered a minute and said, "As far as I'm concerned I only saw one horse."

Carol smiled happily—knowing he was referring to her glorious Eternal Dell.

Buck asked, "Which one was that?"

"Really Rugged."

Carol snapped to attention, surprised by this answer from left field and thought, "What a dumb jerk this guy is. Here I'm showing him my best Quarter Horses and he picks a Thoroughbred!"

Bruised pride drove Carol to speak without her usual regard for diplomacy, "I can't believe that! Why would you pick him?"

The rancher replied with quiet conviction, "Because he's the only horse I saw that looks like he could do it all...and I believe he could."

The next morning when Mann Bailey called, Carol told him, "We sure enjoyed seeing you yesterday. But Mann, please do me a favor and don't bother bringin' that stupid friend of yours here again. He doesn't know where he came from, let alone what he's talking about!"

In retrospect, Carol candidly reports, "Mann and I laughed about it then, but that laugh has turned on me time and again as that "stupid" rancher's words proved out—he had that horse pegged! It's been very humbling for me to realize how wrong I was about him and how right he was about Really Rugged!"

Like the pragmatic pioneers who first developed the Quarter Horse, that wise cattleman's judgment

*Alisa Lark, in 1977, at the All American Quarter Horse Congress where she won both the Open and Youth Versatility Classes. pictured left to right: Chris Manion, Stacy Striegel, and Tommy Manion*

*Alisa Lark and Stacy Striegel*

was not swayed by accepted expectations of breeding alone. He'd tuned in to the individual animal and aptly assessed Really Rugged's unique qualities.

Early ranchers couldn't support a stable full of specialized task horses—most struggled to keep a single horse alive. Thus, a ranch horse was pressed into all kinds of service: one horse to ride, work cattle, pull wagons, plus race for fun and wagers. Two hundred years of breeding for such practical versatility has resulted in today's popular and dependable American Quarter Horse.

One prime example of the breed was Alisa Lark, an All-Around Champion mare whose reputation spread across the country from California in the mid-1970's to enchant fifteen-year-old Stacy Striegel. Having seen Alisa Lark written up in the Quarter Horse Journal, Stacy set her heart and sights on the mare. When Stacy outgrew her current show horse, she reminded her parents of Alisa Lark. By that time however, the mare had disappeared from competition and the Striegels couldn't find her. Months passed...then, on New Year's Day, 1977, at Florida's Gold Coast show, Stacy overheard someone mention Alisa Lark's name and the fact that she was for sale in Southern California.

Contact was made and Stacy, her mom, Mary Kay, and younger sister, Terese, flew to Los Angeles to try Alisa Lark—now being trick-trained by a stuntman who doubled for Marlon Brando. The trainer drove the Striegels in his ancient pickup to a hillside pasture where they found the sixteen-hand, six-year-old brown beauty grazing under the world famous sign proclaiming: HOLLYWOOD. The Striegels had found their star.

Alisa Lark was shipped from balmy California to wintry Bloomington, Illinois, in January. As if that were not enough of an adjustment, her first show with Stacy was in Canada—in February! Since the two were just getting used to one another, Stacy only signed up for three events: Western Pleasure, Western Riding and Trail. They won all three.

Through the years, their partnership proved irresistible. Elegant and athletic, Alisa Lark moved with the fluid grace of a figure skater while her young owner guided her with pride and love through the challenging, varied maneuvers of both English and western classes.

Renowned trainer and judge, Richard Shrake remembers, "Alisa Lark was grace in motion...you could put a teacup between her ears and it would never spill a drop! She was such a soft, balanced mover you couldn't even hear her lope by."

"I judged Alisa Lark at the Quarter Horse Congress, which is the largest horse show in the world. I placed her first, not only in the Western Pleasure, but in the English Hunt Seat. I knew I'd get flack from some saying, 'Hey, they're either western or they're English...not both!' And as a judge I knew it probably wasn't a good thing to do politically. But this mare was such a superior mover that in my heart I couldn't do anything else but let her win both championships—English and Western."

"To me, performance is movement, so it wasn't really hard...those great ones just jump up and knock you down! As I look back, I know it was risky, but I'm still proud of my decision—that mare earned both those championship titles."

For a while Stacy and Alice (her pet name for Alisa Lark) dominated the Youth Division, winning almost sixty All-Arounds, plus many other prestigious titles and classes too numerous to list here.

The 1977 Congress competition was particularly fierce with more than two hundred contestants entered in the Horsemanship Class—the largest number in AQHA history. This was also the only year Alisa Lark was shown in the Adult Versatility Class which she won handily with Tommy and Chris Manion showing her. Then Stacy and Alice stepped up to win the Youth Versatility title...it suddenly seemed that Alisa Lark was unbeatable! That's when things turned ugly.

As we've witnessed on the fields of competition in recent years—from school sports to the lofty heights of the Olympics—when rivalry is ignited by a compulsive need to win, individuals may cross over the line of sanity, morality and legality.

As Stacy led Alisa Lark back to her stall through a swarm of well-wishers congratulating them on yet another Versatility Championship, trainer Tommy Manion, one of his grooms, and two security agents surrounded them in escort. Stacy laughed, "Tommy! This is above and beyond—Alice and I only feel like royalty!"

Tommy smiled weakly as he handed her a piece of paper, saying, "You need to read this; we just found it on Alisa Lark's tack trunk a few minutes ago."

Scrawled on the outside was, *For the Striegels*. Stacy unfolded the note and froze as she read, *Let's see how much horsemanship you can manage with your mare's legs broke. Take your horse out of competition or we will - permanently!*

Stacy looked up at Tommy in disbelief, "Is this a joke? It has to be a joke...a sick joke! Who would ever want to hurt Alice?"

"Well, how many did you just beat in that Versatility Class? We could start there and the number multiplies with each and every win," Tommy replied.

"But that's not what showing's about!" Stacy declared scornfully.

"It is to some. Winning's all that matters to some people and Alisa Lark's got a pretty tight hold on first place. Obviously someone else wants a shot, and if they can't beat her fairly, they'll beat her...physically."

"What should we do?" asked Stacy.

"That's up to you and your family. I've talked with the head of security and he sent over these two guards for now, but we need to tell your mom and decide whether it's worth the risk to continue competing."

After discussions with Tommy and the head of security, Mary Kay made her decision, "If they were trying to scare us, they've succeeded, but they're not going to intimidate us! We're staying put, and Stacy will show Alice tomorrow as planned. We'll find someone to watch Alice's stall overnight. In the meantime, Tommy's Doberman will keep her company—just in case."

The Doberman settled in with Alisa Lark, the security guard promised he'd check as often as possible, and grooms were keeping an eye out. The family's tension eased. With all those precautions, it seemed impossible that anyone could slip into Alisa Lark's stall. But around 8:30 p.m., the quiet barn suddenly filled with a rumbling growl, then vicious barking and sounds of attack. The guard came running just in time to see a man leap backwards out of Alisa Lark's stall, slamming the door shut.

"Who are you, and what are you doing to that horse!" the guard demanded.

"I'm Gene Striegel, and I wasn't doing anything to the horse!" the shaken man replied. "I just arrived from the airport and thought I'd find my family here. I went in to give Alice a pat when that hound from hell attacked! What's that animal doing in there, anyway?"

After checking Mr. Striegel's identification, the relieved guard explained the situation. Mr. Striegel immediately hired a trusted groom to spend the night at Alisa Lark's stall.

The next day proved memorable on all counts: Alisa Lark was

*Alisa Lark and Terese Striegel at the last show before she was retired to Bo-Bett Farm.*

safe, sound and successful once again as she and Stacy claimed another first—in the biggest Horsemanship Class in AQHA history!

Success continued throughout Alisa Lark's career. When Stacy Striegel went off to college, her younger sister, Terese took over the reins. At Florida's 1978 Gold Coast Show, Terese and Alisa Lark were leading in three categories when Terese came down with the flu so badly she had to be rushed to the hospital. Still weak from illness, Terese returned to Alisa Lark the next day to win the Hunter Under Saddle Gold Coast Championship.

After that show, the Striegels retired their beloved mare to be bred at Bo-Bett Farm, secure in the knowledge that Carol Harris would give Alice and her babies the best of care.

It's somehow fitting that Alisa Lark's retirement year, 1978, was the very year the AQHA established the ultimate Quarter Horse performance award: the title of Superhorse. As Alisa Lark's consistent championship record proved, she was really a Superhorse before there was a Superhorse title.

The stage was now set for a singular twist of genetic fate when Alisa Lark, a versatility champion so invincible as to receive a death threat, was bred to Really Rugged, the great-looking stallion with a temperament so obliging that he literally stepped out of the Thoroughbred racing world to drag a calf out of the water. Quarter Horse enthusiasts waited as eagerly as expectant kin to see what crossing these two stars with such a golden heritage would produce.

Carol & Lark – two unique individuals, together they share many of the same qualities – Beauty, Intelligence, the ability to captivate, the fortitude to perservere, and the courage to go where others have never gone. Carol & Lark are friends to all, ambassadors of our breed and AQHA's treasures.

*Peter & Peggy Eofrancesco, Breeders*

Our friendship is like the couch you gave me 40 years ago – It's still comfortable.

Lucy Wilkinson, Your friend

Carol and her horse, Rugged Lark, are legends.
Matlock Rose, Breeder & Trainer

©Cappy Jackson

# Chapter Two
# Field of Diamonds
## *"Calling All Studs!"*

Hormones—tough to live with, impossible to live without. Although she was an incredibly dependable winner in the show arena, Alisa Lark proved to be an incredible oddity in the breeding shed. Once retired to Bo-Bett, with her active showing routine curtailed, Alisa Lark came into season...then never went out! As a result of her continuous heats, breeding was preempted for almost two years. Additionally, all the popular complaints about human PMS pale in comparison to a mare in heat—sweet Alice became a bit of a menstrual nightmare. Like an equine prima dona, she was indignantly touchy about who she'd let handle her. Always partial to Carol, she was eventually moved into the pasture right next to Carol's house where she settled into contentment.

Without the aid of current medications to regulate hormone levels, Carol and the vet were at a loss to correct the mare's condition. The Striegel's reported that Alisa Lark had cycled normally while on the show circuit, so Carol thought it was worth a try to put her back to work in hopes that regular activity would trigger regular cycles...miraculously that worked. Finally, in the spring of 1980, Alisa Lark was successfully bred to Really Rugged, then turned out to pasture to await the arrival of her first foal.

*Majestic Dell - 1973 Quarter Horse Stallion by Eternal Dell and out of Quo Vadis.*

*This jet-black halter stallion's get were shown successfully at halter and performance.*

*Eternal Too -
by Eternal Sun
and out of Debonaire
by Steel Bars.*

*Eternal Too was the 1969
High Point Halter Stallion
and an AQHA Champion.
He sired many halter and
performance champions
for Bo-Bett Farm.*

As Florida's sultry summer days melted into the breezy autumn storm season, disaster struck—colic suddenly and inexplicably took Really Rugged at age twenty-one. A hurricane couldn't have caused a blacker day at Bo-Bett Farm. Saddened by the loss, but always one to celebrate life rather than grieve an animal's death, Carol reflected gratefully on all Really Rugged had given her through the years: many talented and beautiful foals, tremendous personal pride, and a greater appreciation of the Thoroughbred horse.

Since the untimely passing of her wonderful stud left Carol with just three stallions—all carrying the same bloodlines—she was forced to begin the search for another outcross stallion to use on her Eternal Dell, Majestic Dell, and Eternal Too mares. As always, her goal was to produce halter horses that could also perform well in competition. Carol let it be known she was in the market for a stallion—she called many friends and colleagues, checked out horses at shows, and traveled across the country to inspect prospects. Unfortunately, nothing fit her dual halter/performance criteria because the style in halter horses had evolved into heavily muscled, big-hipped animals that could no longer perform with quickness, ease and agility. To make performance horses out of the current halter horses would be like trying to make a track-and-field star out of a sumo-wrestler.

Meanwhile, the 1981 crop of foals began arriving at Bo-Bett in the early spring. Alisa Lark's first born turned out to be a beautifully balanced, healthy colt of unremarkable coloring. Little Rugged Lark was a solid bay with not a white hair on him—no chrome here! The Striegel's were both excited and

Rugged 16 Lark

disappointed with the news. They were thrilled that Alisa Lark had produced a healthy foal at long last, but they'd been hoping for a filly since they didn't want the responsibility of showing a stallion.

Their disappointment deepened knowing that due to his recent death, this would be the only foal by Really Rugged and Alisa Lark. As heir to such aristocratic breeding, this young colt was too valuable to geld, so the Striegel's told Carol to add Rugged Lark to Bo-Bett Farm's sales list and breed Alisa Lark back to Majestic Dell in hopes that she'd deliver their desired filly. As luck would have it, Alisa Lark produced a number of fine fillies for the Striegel's...Rugged Lark turned out to be her only colt.

As she does every year, Carol worked closely with, and carefully evaluated this latest crop of foals. Carol possesses a unique set of judging skills, for second only to her passion for animals is her passion for art. Her college and post-graduate years were spent studying anatomy with famed British equine sculptress, Kathleen Wheeler, and painting at the Art Students League in New York City. Thus, in addition to decades of living and breathing horses, Carol brings the critical eye of a true artist for

*Rugged Lark enjoys his first meal at 20 minutes old.*

*Rugged Lark in 1981 as a suckling with Don McDuffee.*

proportion, balance and beauty to bear in assessing conformation.

While observing the 1981 foals, Carol often found her attention drawn to Alice's Rugged Lark. Like passing a diamond in the dust, her eye kept catching little sparkles of brilliance in the plain bay colt. From the very first, Rugged Lark's natural balance allowed him to move around his mother with precocious elegance. Later, as a weanling, he displayed exceptional athleticism in the pasture running and playing with other colts. He was always curious and friendly—when people came into the pasture, young Rugged Lark would trot over as if to say, "Hey, good to see ya! What's up? Ya wanna play?"

As the months passed, Rugged Lark became more and more of a standout to Carol and she worked hard to find just the right home for him. Photos and information were sent to a number of trainers, breeders and friends. A few even flew in to see Rugged Lark figuring any horse that got Carol Harris excited was well worth seeing firsthand. But when Rugged Lark marked his first birthday at Bo-Bett, there were still no takers for the Striegel's extra-ordinary, ordinary bay colt.

That spring of 1982, the search was still on for an outcross stallion, and Carol was beginning to feel a bit desperate. In eighteen months she'd not found what she wanted. Then she heard about a horse in Texas that sounded promising named Bars Reward. Upon investigation, she liked him a lot...and even better, she loved what he was producing.

She decided to buy him and breathed a sigh of relief that the long outcross-search was now over. But before the sale was finalized, tragedy struck.

"Terribly sorry...Bars Reward died.... These things happen.... Hate it as much as you...a fine horse..."

Carol hung up from that call feeling sad and frustrated. After months of futile effort, the great stallion quest was once again at ground zero. "Horses...one step forward, six steps back," she muttered in exasperation, then thought with a mix of gratitude and guilt, "At least, I hadn't bought him yet."

A few weeks after that fateful phone call, Carol sat up in bed with a start, wrenched from a dream about a book she'd read years ago entitled 'Acres of Diamonds'. The story dealt with the proverbial circumstance of frantically searching far and wide for life's most precious gifts when what you're craving is usually available right at home...once you realize you have acres of diamonds in your own backyard.

"Of course!" shouted Carol, "The horse I've been searching for is right here, in my own backyard...Rugged Lark!" Eureka! The positive certainty of her realization seemed as right and exhilarating as John Sutter's discovery of gold in his mill stream.

Carol checked the clock to see how soon she could call the Striegel's... 3:32, way too early. Go back to sleep...not possible. Carol turns on the light to read, dozes, awakens...4:12, reads some more,

*Rugged Lark as a yearling.*
*The extraordinary, ordinary bay colt was not very remarkable - yet.*

dozing, awakens...4:54, change position, punch the pillow, try to sleep...sleep...awake, 5:23...still dark. Will this night never end! ...sky's lightening...6:07. Carol gets up, showers, dresses, feeds and checks her dogs.

7:15 a.m. "It's a work day, they should be up," Carol rationalizes as she dials the Striegel's number. Terese answers.

"Hey, Terese, it's Carol Harris."

"Oh, hi, Carol.... Is everything all right?"

"Yes, I'm sorry to call so early, but I wanted to let you know I just sold your colt.

"Oh, Mom will be so pleased. What did you get for him?

"Just what she wanted—$15,000."

"And he's going to a good home?"

"I think so. He's staying right here with me."

Terese laughed, "That's not a good home, Carol, that's a fabulous home! Mom will be thrilled. Actually, here she is...."

Sharing the excitement of her nocturnal revelation with Mary Kay, Gene and Terese Striegel, gave Carol a rush of confident relief bordering on euphoria. Never before had a decision felt so right. It was as if she'd been instructed by someone outside herself that this was meant to be. As a result, every fiber of her being was certain she was on the right path. Suddenly Carol relaxed into the comfort of faith—that rare inner peace and conviction that walks hand-in-hand with destiny.

With renewed energy, she charged down to the barn to admire the shining diamond-in-the-rough she'd just picked up in her own backyard. She was eager to begin the challenging process of polishing and finishing Rugged Lark into a multi-faceted, gleaming gem of a show horse.

Probably the only conflict that's ever occurred between Lark and Carol was deciding which wine to serve in that classic picture.
Walter & Nancy Hughes, Breeders, Trainer & Judge

Diana, the Princess of Wales, was often referred to as "The People's Princess". That is how I have come to think of Rugged Lark - "The People's Horse". Carol made him accessible to everyone and they all could imagine a Lark in their life. I am honored to have known them.
Leslie Sowder Baker - Former AQHA Coordinator

The feeling of confidence I get when I ride Rugged Lark is one that I will never forget. He has a natural-born instinct to please, better than any horse I have ever ridden.

Chris Cox, trainer

# Chapter Three
# Spinning To Destiny
### "The Launch and a Flameout"

The process of making and molding world-class show animals is Carol Harris' life's blood. With the exception of a few years in art school, the focus of nearly every waking moment of her life has been spent learning and perfecting this process. As a result, Carol has developed a very personal, hands-on method for producing healthy, happy horses. Since that process actually starts long before an animal is born, she insists that things be done right from the start:

Initially, astute breeding decisions mark a Bo-Bett baby with Carol's stamp from the very point of conception. Then, recognizing the importance of prenatal care coupled with the enormous responsibility of caring for another's beloved horse, Carol makes sure all broodmares receive diligent attention.

As foaling time approaches, mares are closely monitored. Since they often foal in the darkest hours of morning, and births happen rapidly, Carol instituted an unusual incentive program. If a barn attendant alerted Carol in time to race—often in her pajamas—from her bed to the barn and reach the mare before the foal arrived, the attendant received a monetary "foaling bonus".

Alisa Lark's attendant was one who earned his bonus in 1981. Not only was Carol present when Alisa Lark's foal arrived, she had her camera ready to record the momentous event for the Striegel family anxiously awaiting in Illinois.

Although helpful, the attendant-alert system was never 100% effective, so in the late 1970's, Carol was among the first breeders to install an innovative video monitoring system. With cameras in the foaling stalls and a monitor in her bedroom, Carol was now also able to keep an eye on expectant mares throughout the night during foaling season.

Today Bo-Bett also relies on the

*Rugged Lark says "hello"*
*to the world at twenty minutes old*

*(top photo) The paddock for broodmares at Bo-Bett Farm. In the background is the broodmare barn and office.*

*(bottom photo) Yearling prospects in the pasture at Bo-Bett Farm.*

high-tech dependability of the Foal Alert® system by which the mare is physically wired so at the onset of foaling activity an electronic signal instantly rings ten phones at the farm— including those at Wendy's and Carol's bedsides.

As is the practice at Bo-Bett, Alice and her foal were kept in their own stall and paddock for the first couple of weeks after birth. This precaution allows the foal's eyesight and instincts to develop to the point that it is able to pick its own mother out of the herd. Only then, with the danger of a newborn getting kicked by a strange mare thus diminished, are the mare and foal turned out with other nursing pairs.

Pastures at Bo-Bett are laid out in spacious ten, twenty and thirty-acre parcels allowing plenty of grazing, as well as safe relief distances should equine disputes arise. Herd relationships are monitored, and if two mares don't get along, one is moved to a new paddock or pasture until all settle in compatibly.

It is during this time spent in broodmare bands that foals learn many vital lessons in horse and herd behavior. At about four or five months of age, suckling foals are weaned and move down the road toward independent living. Since weaning is emotionally stressful for both foals and mares, Carol works to minimize that stress as much as possible—even consulting the signs of the zodiac to determine the most favorable time for the separation.

Each weanling is put then in an individual stall where it learns to eat, drink and sleep on its own. Later, they are turned out together for comfort and to gain socialization skills, learn to react to herd dynamics, play games, run, enjoy mock fights and generally grow to be strong, agile, well-adjusted horses.

An important part of a foal's schooling at Bo-Bett is experience with people. Although Carol works with all the foals as much as possible, she can't do it all, so she carefully selects, trains and supervises assistants who share her most fundamental philosophy. Each and every animal is treated with respect, love and trust because Carol believes an animal gives back like behaviors to its handler—if you give love, it will return love; give trust, it will return trust. Rugged Lark grew up in the warm logic of this belief.

As a suckling, Lark was gently introduced to human handling: rubbed all over, taught to lead, have his feet trimmed.... As a weanling, he showed the usual anxiety when Alisa Lark was lead away, but his trust in people helped him adjust quickly. Soon he was at home in the stall on his own, quiet when being washed in a noisy spray of water, and enjoying lessons in the round-pen with his first trainer, Don McDuffee. Naturally calm around people, this consistently gentle handling afforded Rugged Lark the temperament of a friendly lap dog where humans are concerned. To paraphrase Will Rogers, "he's never met a man he didn't like."

*A Bo-Bett foal being handled by capable assistants.*

Rugged Lark had been on Bo-Bett's sales list for more than a year when Carol had her fateful middle-of-the-night-wake-up-call and bought him herself. The following month, her good friend Richard Shrake was in town judging a local show. Carol shanghaied him after the last event of the day—which had run late into the evening.

"Richard, you've got to come by the farm and see my new stud," she declared excitedly, "He's something special."

"Carol, ordinarily I'd love to, but I'm so hungry right now I'll collapse in a coma if I don't get something to eat. It's late, I'm whipped, I have to be back here for an 8:00 class in the morning...and I sure don't need to see another horse right now."

"Oh, quit complaining," Carol cajoled amicably, "I just want you to see this one because Rugged Lark is not just another horse...he's by Really Rugged out of Alisa Lark."

Richard perked up. "Alisa Lark's colt?"

"Yup." said Carol.

*"The second he moved, the hair on my neck stood up,"
a quote from Richard Shrake.*

"Okay, dinner first, then the barn....your treat."

"It's a deal! I know just where we can go—there's little place on the way that's real popular with the locals—it's actually world famous," Carol grinned as she took Richard by the arm and escorted him to her pickup.

"I hope this horse is more of a treat than dinner was. I've never heard McDonald's referred to as a 'world-famous restaurant' before." Richard joked as they headed for the farm.

It was almost 11:00 when they pulled in at Bo-Bett. Carol switched on high beams and parked the truck to illuminate Rugged Lark's paddock. Seeing Carol's pride and joy standing there, Richard's first thought was, 'uh, oh.... Nice looking, but he's Thoroughbred-y; not big and bulky, it's going to be real hard to get his halter points.'

Then Rugged Lark moved off....

"The second he moved, the hair on my neck stood up," said Richard. "It was magic. That horse just barely touched the ground, and when he went from a walk to a lope his topline didn't move. His legs were slow, he had the flat knees, his hocks were just like a pendulum...and such balance! It was a thrill to watch him—even at that age. He'd inherited his father's good looks and his mother's poetic motion. I immediately thought, 'Wow, no problem...he's a performance horse!'

"Well, you're definitely a better judge of horseflesh than you are of dining spots, Carol," Richard said, grinning. "You're going to have fun with this one...he is special and I wouldn't have wanted to miss this. Thanks for the treat."

Although she'd always loved halter horses and had great fun and success showing them, Carol felt the

*(top right photo)* Majestic Justice - Champion Florida Halter Horse 4 years in a row.

*(top left photo)* Eternal Striker by Eternal Dell - Winner of 80 Halter Points & 743 Performance Points.

*(bottom photo)* Eternal Class - A winner in both halter and pleasure.

competitive standard was rapidly evolving to a point of excessive muscle and bulk. So she decided to head down a different path, and from the day she purchased Rugged Lark, she started planning. From now on, her primary focus would be performance horses. "But," she thought, "they damn sure better be pretty!"

As a long yearling approaching his second birthday, Rugged Lark was turned over to Bo-Bett's new reining trainer, Mike Corrington, who was amazed by how quickly this particular youngster caught on. "Rugged Lark learned so quick; you'd just show him something one time and that was it. I could almost hear him say, 'Well, I got that, what's next?' He made my job very easy."

Mike was not only impressed by the colt's quick mind, he was intrigued by an odd habit he had. "The most unique thing about Rugged Lark when he was young was the way he'd stand off by himself and watch other colts play. He had a real unusual way of holdin' his head—down and cocked—observing them intently like he was studyin' their behavior.... I've never seen another horse do that before or since."

That young horse got Mike thinking a lot about equine intelligence...working

*(top photo) Carol Harris and AQHA inspector Jim Wright*

*(bottom photo) Rugged Lark and Mike Corrington*

with Rugged Lark convinced him there's more to it than most people know or are willing to acknowledge. As Mike explains, "By him bein' so easy to get along with, I could allow him to use his own mind and natural talents. For instance, I didn't have to teach him how to change leads, I just taught him to change leads when I wanted him to. I didn't have to teach him to turn around, all I did was teach him when I wanted him to turn around. We didn't have to teach him how to do anything, I just added cues to aid his own abilities because it was all there naturally."

"Then with his mind bein' so agreeable all the time there was never a conflict. He trusted us, and we trusted him—it was kind of a fifty-fifty deal. From the very beginning we had no reason to mistrust him and he had no reason to mistrust us."

Early training also highlighted Rugged Lark's exceptional temperament since he displayed none of the confusion or anxiety that most colts experience with initial schooling. Like a camera to his soul, Rugged Lark's large, soft eye reflected only his curious intelligence, eagerness to please and the gentle calm that grows out of the security in knowing how to respond to the trainer's requests and cues. Much like an honor student who's always confidently prepared in class, Rugged Lark clearly enjoyed learning, respected his teachers, tried hard to do what was asked of him, and usually succeeded—with distinction.

Because Rugged Lark's outrageously responsive rides always put him in such a good mood, it wasn't long before Mike began saving his favorite student for the last training

©Kerry Heubeck

*Rugged Lark and Mike Corrington getting down to the business of reining.*

session of the day—then every workday ended on a delightful high note, "It was just a joy to ride Rugged Lark because he never disappointed me. He was always in a good mood, so I always rode him last because I knew when I quit, I'd be in a good mood, too."

Mike hauled the talented young colt to shows to give him exposure and occasionally showed him in Western Pleasure classes. Since Rugged Lark's breeding labeled him an Appendix Quarter Horse, the first important hurdle in his career was to pass inspection for conformation and breed type in order to be registered as a Quarter Horse. Rugged Lark quickly received his Register of Merit in Western Pleasure, and after a visit from AQHA inspector Jim Wright in 1983, was accepted into the Permanent Quarter Horse Registry.

Rugged Lark obviously thought Western Pleasure was a piece of cake, for in addition to his Register of Merit he earned a Superior rating in that event after just ten shows. Being such a naturally balanced mover, Mike recognized Rugged Lark as a great reining prospect. Now, with his registry in place, it was

*(opposite page) Rugged Lark and Mike Corrington are pictured winning the NRHA Pre-Futurity.*

time to get down to the business of reining....

The first big test would be the 1984 Reining Pre-Futurity in Louisville, Kentucky, with Carol's good friend, renowned horse-show announcer, Keith Bradley, covering the event. Keith has developed a signature broadcasting style to indicate the top score in an event. When the crowd hears Keith's hallmark intonation—his voice slides up as he strings out the word "Thheee" then hesitates before hitting the word, "score"—the audience knows they've just seen the new high-point leader. In tight competition, just the up-slide on that first word is enough to ignite cheers of celebration from the crowd.

With almost eighty three-year-olds competing, this Pre-Futurity was going to require a lot more than beginner's luck. Carol recalls, "Mike had prepared Rugged Lark beautifully. He walked in the arena just like he owned it and did everything effortlessly. He was very correct and flat in his spins, and even though he'd had very little experience stopping, he slid like a champ three times. His rollbacks were pure and he ran his circles just like he was at home. It was all done so easily, yet with such elegance and finesse...it was a breath-taking performance for a young horse."

The judges were impressed and Keith announced, "Thheee....score for number 17, Rugged Lark, ridden by Mike Corrington, 223 on that ride." The crowd roared approval, wowed by what they'd just witnessed. In that single, fluid performance embellished by a competitive maturity well beyond his years, Rugged Lark won more than the event, he won the admiration of the audience and instantly became the favorite for the Congress Reining Futurity. His career was launched in grand style.

Like doting relatives, Bob Standish, Executive Director of the United States Equestrian Team notes, "Of course, all of us in the Quarter Horse business knew about his mother, Alisa Lark, and we were obviously anxious to see what she had produced by Really Rugged."

And now they knew. The seeds of Rugged Lark's legend were sown....

The next important venue was the world's biggest horse show in Columbus, Ohio. The All American Quarter Horse Congress is a city unto itself with an energetic population many times greater than most of the towns in which the thousands of attendees live. The sheer size, bustling activity and electric atmosphere of this show can test the mettle of seasoned horses, and it's a monumental trial for the young ones.

As the winner and odds-on favorite from the Pre-Futurity, Reining was obviously Rugged Lark's competitive future, so he was nominated for the Reining Futurity at the Congress. But Carol's instincts were nudging her to have "an ace in the hole". Since Lark also showed promise in the Hunt Seat events, Carol nominated Rugged Lark in the Reining Futurity for his career and in the Hunt Seat Futurity for good measure.

Out of almost two hundred entries, Rugged Lark drew a great position in the first go-round of the Reining Futurity—third from last. As the competition drew to a close, the crowds remained, waiting for the horse that had won Louisville.

Among the interested throng was Richard Shrake who'd stopped by the announcer's booth to visit with his friend Keith Bradley. Keith was busy announcing, so Richard nodded a greeting, then helped himself to a can of peanuts on the desk while he waited for Keith to finish. Prying the top off, he popped a handful into his mouth and munched away. Instantly Richard's eyes bugged out, his mouth flew open in a strangled cry and he spat out peanuts like a gatling gun!

Keith switched off his mike and laughed, "Well, howdy to you, too, Richard! I see you're enjoyin' my

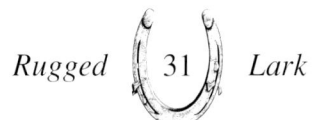

Hotter-than-Hades-Jalapeno-Peanuts."

"Waa, waa, waater...," gasped Richard, "You son-of-a-gun...whaddya leave those things lying around for?"

As he handed him a glass of water, Keith said, "They're a gift from a buddy who keeps me supplied with Planters peanuts rolled in jalapeno pepper dust. I'd challenged him 'cuz last time they weren't hot enough. I haven't had a chance to taste these yet, but it looks like he got it right this time."

Just then, an excited murmur caught their attention...Rugged Lark was at the in-gate.

Still nursing the glass of water, Richard turned toward the arena as Keith declared, "Exhibitor 231, Rugged Lark, owned by Carol Harris, Mike Corrington riding." Suddenly, anticipation triggered total silence.

Horse and rider move forward confidently—relaxed and ready. With the grace of a dancer, Rugged Lark responded to Mike's invisible cues as they loped picture-perfect circles, stopped and spun beautifully...Rugged Lark was laying a beautiful, seamless pattern and Mike realized what a super go they were having.

Then the unthinkable happened. Like the tiny blip on a radar screen, Mike's concentration flickered just an instant as he asked Rugged Lark for one last spin and his student dutifully delivered....

As soon as they completed that fourth rotation, Mike heard a loud groan rise from the crowd. Only then did he realize what he'd done—he'd failed to count rotations—the pattern called for three! In that fourth perfect revolution, all was lost.

Horrified, Mike finished the run, knowing he had blown the pattern. His star pupil had performed faultlessly yet they were now disqualified because Mike got carried away for a fraction of a second. In that single revolution, pilot error turned Rugged Lark's stellar career launch into a flameout.

Across the arena, Keith Bradley saw the look of disbelief strike Carol like a head shot. Her hands flew up to her face as she fell back against her seat. Taking a ragged, deep breath, she then gathered her things and headed for the out-gate as reality hit her a second time through the loudspeakers, "Thank you. The score for #231, Rugged Lark, ridden by Mike Corrington...Zero."

As she strode to the arena, Carol tried to think of what she could possibly say to Mike.... All that came to mind were pathetic platitudes: 'Win some, lose some' or 'Better luck next time'....

None seemed to fit because there's really nothing you can say to lessen the sting of loss due to an obvious error. This was just one of those things that can happen in the stress and emotion of competition. Then she remembered something she'd heard years ago, "God always gives us more practice at losing than winning because that's the tougher lesson to learn."

Carol never got to deliver that enlightened message. When she arrived at the out-gate, she found a stranger holding her horse. Without a word Mike had dropped Rugged Lark at the gate, walked out of the arena...and out of Lark's life.

"I had the pleasure of spending the winter of 1984 at Bo-Bett. Lark was three and training for the NRHA Futurity. I never saw him again until last winter - except in his stall at Equitana and Congress. I had the opportunity to visit Bo-Bett again early in 2000. I arrived in mid-afternoon to find Lark turned out in his paddock looking as bright and beautiful as he did at three, the only difference I could see was more muscle. Rugged Lark's career has been special to so many. I enjoyed riding his sire, Really Rugged, in some races in New York in the sixties. He was smaller than Lark, but very pretty and he could run."

John Rotz,
Hall of Fame jockey and NCHA exhibitor

# Chapter Four
# The Hunt for Plan B
### *"Get Right Back On..."*

Carol had no time to go looking for Mike. The only other event Rugged Lark was entered in, the Hunt Seat Futurity, was coming up in less than an hour. If Rugged Lark had placed well in the Reining Futurity, Carol had planned to scratch him from the hunt-seat event. But when his first reining go-round suddenly become his last, the Hunt Seat Futurity took on greater significance.

Years of riding and showing had taught Carol some valuable life lessons: when you're thrown, get right back on; and in competition, as in life, there are no guarantees. If one plan is dashed, don't waste precious time whining, get back in the saddle and head for the next goal. It pays to be flexible and have an ace in the hole—a "Plan B"—to fall back on.

With so little time between the two events, Carol shifted into high gear and "got back on" with the current Plan B—the Hunt Seat Futurity. She ran Lark to the blacksmith shop to have the reiners' sliding plates taken off his hind feet, then went in search of Lynn Palm to let her know they would be competing after all.

Thankfully, she found Lynn almost immediately, "I guess we're going to the Hunt Seat Futurity...have you got your clothes here?" Lynn nodded and rushed off to change into proper gear while Carol retrieved Lark. No time to reset shoes on his hind feet, he needed to get his mane

*Rugged Lark is pictured winning the Three-Year-Old Hunter Under Saddle Futurity at the 1984 All American Quarter Horse Congress with Lynn Palm aboard.*

*Rugged Lark in 1984 after winning
the Florida Royal Hunter Under Saddle Futurity*

braided and have his western tack switched to English.
Somehow it all got done but there wasn't even time for a warm-up before their section was called.

Watching Lynn and Lark from the in-gate, Carol was struck by the metamorphosis that took place before her eyes. Now Rugged Lark didn't even look like a western reining horse—the mount in this arena was all English. A well-turned-out conformation hunter: elegant, soft and even, performing extensions, collections, and transitions as smooth as a Rolls Royce transmission. The transformation was much more than just a change of tack; it was a complete change of demeanor. Like a talented method actor, Rugged Lark seemed to consciously alter his way of going, taking on the very character of the discipline in which he was competing. As a result, Lynn and Rugged Lark won both go-rounds and the finals to make an impressive clean sweep of the 1984 Three-Year-Old Congress Hunt Seat Futurity!

Like the Phoenix rising from the ashes to once again fly with eagles, Rugged Lark's introduction at the 1984 All American Quarter Horse Congress instantly changed from devastation to jubilation. Both futurities had brought startlingly unexpected results—disqualification, then miraculous victory.

In witnessing Lark's striking transformation, Carol began to grasp that Lark's real genius lies in the remarkable intelligence, natural balance, and willing attitude that allows him to perform with an uncanny level of comprehension that goes well beyond practiced action. This horse seems to truly understand what each rider needs from him, then delivers the goods like a pro.

It is extremely difficult for one horse to excel in both Western and English disciplines since the events are as different as the cultures which developed them: the hard scrabble of America's working-class ranchland vs. the ritualistic propriety of British aristocracy.

Reining, roping, cutting, trail and even western pleasure grew out of skills needed to work cattle and cover miles of territory in as easy and comfortable a manner as possible for the cowboy in the saddle. Over the years, specific athletic abilities have evolved for each of these events through selection and breeding. Reiners are bred for a willing response to athletic maneuvers; ropers need the sprinter's explosive speed while cutters must be agile with cow savvy.

Currently, the style of western pleasure horses seems to have little purpose. They demand an extremely slow pace at the walk, jog and lope with such a low headset that some are even called "peanut rollers". Their movement hardly resembles the functional ranch horses who made a cowboy's endless work rewarding and pleasant.

Among many in the AQHA who hope the current extremes in western pleasure will revert back to a more natural presentation is Carol Harris. She openly declares, "I'm sick and tired of these horses looking so unhappy, and I'm sick of my non-Quarter-Horse friends making fun of our western pleasure classes."

*Carol Harris on Hollywood Joan cutting at Devon, Pennsylvania*

"The pleasure horse was originally the ranch horse used to mend fence and doctor cattle," Carol explains. "On the way home after a day's work, a cowboy would hit a little jog for five or six miles back to the ranch, or take a soft lope letting his horse's head hang naturally low. This horse had been worked all day and was both tired and relaxed. That's the comfortable Quarter Horse everybody wanted to ride. The western pleasure class was a contest developed for this kind of horse. If they were good, they were natural—no one tried to manufacture them. Now it seems we turn them out like cloned sheep.

*Carol Harris and Hollywood Joan, in 1962, receiving The Maryland-Virginia Cutting Championship Trophy from Mrs. Byron Mathews*

"I once had a mare called Hollywood Joan that was a cutting horse with a lot of energy. I had to ride her a lot before I cut on her, otherwise she'd buck on her first cow—she'd be headin' a cow and buckin' at the same time. It used to drive me crazy, but rather than just lope endless circles on her to work her down before cutting, I started riding her in pleasure classes to take a little sting out of her. Joan was an extremely cute, naturally low-headed mare with a lot of expression. Soon she started winning those pleasure classes left and right—not because she was highly trained or intimidated, but because she epitomized what western horses were meant to be."

"Somewhere along the way a lot of things changed. It wasn't all bad, a lot of it was good and the popularity of the American Quarter Horse went out of sight. But as competition grew, we got very hard on our horses and naturally some trainers got harder than others. "Excessive" is the word that always seems to come to my mind."

"I remember how a bunch of us would sit in the stands at horse shows during a lunch recess watching certain trainers working their horses. We'd place bets on how many times each guy would jerk his horse's head in one circle of the ring."

"I'll bet 16."

"No, I say, 25."

"Then we'd all put up a quarter.... It got that bad, it was ridiculous. One guy was the recognized champion; we called him 'Captain Bad Ass'."

"It got to where these guys couldn't even sit on a horse and talk to you without messin' with their horses' heads, snatchin' on a rein—over and over.... Like watching a horse cribbing—half the time they weren't even aware they were doing it! But I have to admit these guys were card-carrying, bonafide horse trainers 'cause they could make a horse do just about anything...they certainly discovered how to make a horse go slow!"

"As it stands now, in order to be competitive, a horse has to match the same unnatural templates promoted by trainers who keep pushing the limits simply to show how much they can get out of a horse. But I sincerely believe Quarter Horse judges and trainers will wake-up and reverse this trend of artificial extremes before the essence of the animal we love is destroyed."

In conclusion Carol offers this hopeful solution, "A little more forward motion in our Western Pleasure horses would probably remedy everything. Then our judges could concentrate on movement, our riders could concentrate on enjoyment, our horses could concentrate on being natural, and our spectators could concentrate on what the word "pleasure" really means."

*Rugged Lark as a Two-Year-Old Western Pleasure Horse on his way to his superor title.*

As a result of the distinctly different ways of going between the western and English hunt-seat events, it is very difficult for one horse to excel in both disciplines. As Keith Bradley observes, "There are very few horses capable of doing a nice, smooth job at Western Pleasure that can then pick up their head and carriage well enough to win at Hunt Seat. A horse trained to show Western—especially today—where we've got a jog that's just about a normal walk, and a lope that...I don't know how they can get a horse to lope so slow...to then come back and show in proper English form? It's close to impossible."

Yet, as a two- and a three-year-old, Rugged Lark did just that—proving he is that rarity of rarities—a natural.

"One of Rugged Lark's exceptional strengths in showing," Keith continues, "is that you tack him up as a Western Pleasure horse, he's a Western Pleasure horse. You put him in English tack and he kinda picks himself up—like puttin' a tux on a dude—his whole being changes. He looks the part, then acts the part like he's been born to it!"

Awed by the versatile proficiency displayed by her extra-ordinary bay colt, Carol became fascinated by the possibilities his naturally diverse talents represented. An exceptional reining horse, now a hunt-seat futurity champion...what more could this young horse do? "Plan B" had opened the door to a whole new world of possibilities for Carol and Rugged Lark.

When they had arrived at the Congress, Mike and Carol had wanted Rugged Lark to make his mark as a Reining horse. Now, due to another unexpected twist of fate, she had put him in another championship arena. Suddenly, her mind snapped back to the death of Bars Reward—another disappointment that had proven prophetic. In that situation, Rugged Lark turned out to be her 'Plan B'. Now, an overspin had forced another Plan B—the Hunt-Seat Futurity—through which she'd discovered Rugged Lark's inherently versatile abilities. Was it possible that the Reining Futurity disqualification wasn't a failure, but rather once again, the hand of fate on the rein, guiding Carol's direction with Rugged Lark? Could it be showing her that Rugged Lark is the legendary Quarter Horse that can do it all...and do it all at championship level?

The legend takes hold....

Dear Carol A. Harris,
I was so excited at the Congress when I got to touch Lark. This may sound stupid but I always dream of riding him.
Sincerely,
Brooke Darmstadt, 12 years old, Texas

Dear Carol Harris,
I'm looking forward to visiting you and Rugged Lark. Please tell him I'm coming.
Your friend,
Megan Quigley, Iowa

©Sara Gentry

# Chapter Five
# A Matter of Trust...and Love
### "Championship Philosophy"

*(top photo) Bo-Bett's Trophy Room*

*(bottom photo) Carol's longtime best friend, Isabel Robson, with one of her champion harness ponies.*

The single largest room at Bo-Bett Farm is not its office nor Carol's generous parlor—it's the trophy room. Reminiscent of a pirate's treasure trove, it has to be big to hold Bo-Bett's business booty. Floor-to-ceiling glass cabinets display gleaming silver bowls, plaques and championship trophies. Scattered on the expansive polished conference table in the room's center are dozens of tooled-leather scrapbooks and photo albums filled to bursting with feature articles, magazine covers and mementos chronicling the accomplishments of Bo-Bett champions. Circling overhead, just below the ceiling cornice, is a cavalcade of "iron ponies": matched golden and silver statuettes representing literally hundreds of grand championships.

In lieu of decorative paper, the walls are covered with awards, citations, proclamations, and paintings honoring Bo-Bett's most famous sires: Eternal Dell, Really Rugged, Jay's Sugar Bars, Majestic Dell, Eternal Too, Majestic Justice, Rugged Lark....

For nearly fifty years, Carol Harris has operated a full-service show facility to breed, raise, train, show and sell the best horses—and dogs—she knows how to produce. Yes, dogs, too. The phenomenal success she's enjoyed in the equine world is mirrored by equal success in the canine world.

Showing dogs actually preceded her

*(pictured above) Ch. Coventry Queue, owned by Isabel Robson, is pictured with handler, Michael Scott, winning the Herding Group at Westminster Kennel Club.*

*(pictured left) Ch. Lake Cove's That's My Boy, owned by Isabel Robson, is pictured with handler, Dennis McCoy, winning the Non-Sporting Group at Westminster Kennel Club.*

horse-showing career by a few years. In 1934, inspired by a notice in Dog World magazine advertising an up-coming show in nearby South Orange, New Jersey, ten-year-old Carol, along with her best friend and neighbor, Isabel Prizer, entered their family pets: Isabel's English Setter, Spot, and Carol's Collie, Rex. In preparing their animals for excellence, the girls took a tip from special treatments their mothers received at the nearby Charles of the Ritz Beauty Salon—the hot-oil wrap.

Two days prior to the show, Carol and Isabel lifted a gallon jug of imported olive oil from Carol's mother's pantry and doused both dogs. Twelve shampoos later, the poor dogs still looked like greased monkeys. The day of the show, the two youngsters called a taxi cab and headed off with Rex and Spot. Though they won no ribbons that day, both girls were bitten by the show bug and hooked for life. Just like Carol, Isabel Prizer—better known today as Isabel Robson—has made an impressive mark in both canine and equine show circles having owned the top Pointer, Standard Poodle, Dalmatian and Corgi in the country, as well as champion harness, saddle horses and hackney ponies. To this day, the two remain best of friends still sharing their passion for dogs and horses—only now on a wildly successful professional level.

From the 1940's on, Carol has bred and shown a large variety of breeds including German Shepherds, Scotties, Dobermans, and Dalmatians. Now specializing in Whippets and Italian Greyhounds, she's bred well over two hundred champion Whippets and her Italian Greyhounds are

(pictured left) Italian Greyhound, Ch. Bo-Bett's Perry Peridot, one of Carol's many top-winning show dogs.

(pictured below) Carol's Italian Greyhound stud dog, Dario. Dario has sired an outrageous number of champions, more than any other sire in the history of the breed!

Dario's portrait was painted by Ocala artist, Debbie Fitzgerald.

Carol has approximately sixty dogs at home. They all know their names and <u>most</u> of them come when they are called.

"I can't imagine life without dogs" - Carol Harris

almost impossible to beat. Carol's Italian Greyhound stud dog, Dario, has sired an outrageous number of champions—93—more than any other sire in the history of the breed!

As Carol's longtime friend, Sue Page notes, "Because she's an artist who understands the correctness of form, she knows how a dog is supposed to look for each particular breed. Therefore she knows what she wants to achieve, then breeds to get that correctness...she works so hard at it, everything she does turns to gold."

Bo-Bett's most illustrious equine and canine sires are celebrated with portraits painted by local artist, Debbie Fitzgerald, who describes her initial visit to Carol's solicitous household: "The first time I was at Carol's home, as we passed by the whelping room, I looked in and saw what I thought was a fur rug. But then a head popped up and I jumped realizing it was just an ordinary rug covered end-to-end, corner-to-corner with puppies! I'll never know how Carol keeps all those dogs straight. She names every dog herself and makes sure each gets what it needs."

Carol's animals are healthy, happy and—even though she has more than sixty dogs at home—each gets individual attention plus custom care and feeding. Sue Page is equally impressed, "Carol can probably afford to hire as many people as she'd need to care for her home and animals, yet she does most of it herself. She wants things done her way, so often it's best for her to do it. She doesn't even own a dishwasher—never has—in this day and age she still hand washes her own dishes!

"She gets up early in the morning and takes care of all those dogs—feeds them and inspects them personally. And she's right there with her horses, too, involved in the training, the showing, and cleaning the stalls if needed. She is one of the most hands-on people involved in livestock that I've ever been around and I believe that's why she's so successful."

"There's plenty to do at Bo-Bett," notes Carol. "But whenever I need a little jump-start, I think of

*(bottom left) Carol says, "Whippets are the best kept secret in dogs." Her champion stud dog, "Royce", is in the top left corner of the photo.*

*(bottom right) Italian Greyhound, Ch. Bo-Bett's Mister Bubbles*

the slogan my New Mexican friend, Jimmie Randals, used when he was promoting his great stallion, Poco Dell, 'You can't do business sitting on your ass.' Jimmie's poetic philosophy always gets me going."

In addition to champion dogs and horses, Carol has also raised three world-class winners of her very own at Bo-Bett: Jeffrey, Allison and Wendy Winans all grew up on the show circuit collecting more than their share of ribbons and trophies. While each takes an active interest in the business, Jeff and Wendy work full-time at Bo-Bett keeping it the efficient, productive, profitable facility it is. The fact that family members live and work so well together sounds almost miraculous in this age of dysfunctional family life. Not only is this family notably functional, the accent is usually put on fun.

As a result, visiting Bo-Bett is a bit like entering Barnum & Bailey's big top. Eager guests stream in and out, happy packs of lithe, multi-colored dogs race around the grounds, in the paddocks frisky foals dance around their dams while yearlings romp in the sun, and at center ring we have the star performer—Rugged Lark—bowing to fans, posing for photos, and sealing deals in the office.

In the office? Yup. Due to Lark's even temperament and the trusted communication between him and Carol, he's often brought into the office for novelty shots or entertaining. Now this is the same office described above...filled with glass shelves and trophy cases in which a less composed stallion could create havoc akin to the fabled bull in a china shop.

Carol has naturally winning ways with all sorts of animals and people and one of her favorite jobs at Bo-Bett is welcoming the many visitors who come to the farm–especially the busloads of

©Reg Corkum

©unknown

*Carol's Children -*
*(top photo)* Jeffrey Winans
*(middle photo)* Wendy Winans with Lark and Carol
*(bottom photo)* Allison Winans-Gaisford

*Rugged Lark carefully admires trophies on glass shelves in the Bo-Bett office.*

school children.

In 1992 she was escorting a class of Professor Anthony Borton's agriculture students from the University of Massachusetts around Bo-Bett when they noticed an abandoned eagle's nest in a tall pine tree at the back corner of Lark's paddock. The professor launched into a discussion on the habits of eagles and surmised that it had probably moved on to better hunting grounds when food became scarce.

"It was wonderful having the eagle here" said Carol. "Unfortunately the nest's been empty for a long time now; we haven't seen it for weeks."

"That's too bad," said the professor. "Eagles are so impressive, it would have been a rare treat to see one up close."

Never one to allow disappointment to take root, Carol joked, "Well, perhaps that old bird's still around...I'll just give him a call."

*Rugged Lark, in the office at Bo-Bett, helping to book the mares that will be coming to see him.*

*Neither Lark nor Carol enjoy filing...*

*...but they love talking on the telephone.*

©TAG Photographics

*Then she turned away, cupped her hands to her mouth and shouted,
"Here eagle! Here eagle, eagle, eagle..."
"This event blew my mind," Carol says.*

Then she turned away, cupped her hands to her mouth and shouted, "Here eagle! Here eagle, eagle, eagle..."

With that, everyone started laughing.

Before Carol even had time to look amazed, a huge bald eagle swooped down from way across the field and landed on the branch of a nearby tree!

Professor Borton exclaimed, "Didn't I tell you she has a way with animals?"

"I couldn't believe it!" says Carol. "That bird had been gone for weeks, so when I saw that damn eagle coming at us, I nearly fell through the ground!"

That eagle may have blown Carol's mind, but it's just another example of animal magic at the daily Bo-Bett circus...

It could be that students are Carol's favorite visitors because she values education so much. Even with her tremendous talents, natural instincts and years of success, Carol actively pursues her own personal extension course of continuing education in conversations with other professionals and horse lovers, at every class of every show she gets near. She is always observing, thinking, analyzing, appreciating...learning.

As her friend, Sue Page, notes, "The last couple of years Carol hasn't had Lark on Stallion Avenue at the Congress, but she's there first thing in the morning anyway. Often there are three arenas going at once and Carol is somewhere watching all the time...even trail, which some consider a chore to watch. Carol loves it because she knows what it takes to train a good trail horse. She appreciates a good trail horse, a good halter horse, a good barrel horse.... She stays up watching the jumping until midnight, then she's back the next morning watching all the hunter classes that go forever and ever...all the bad ones, all the good ones, she's there because she absolutely loves and truly appreciates what a horse can do...any horse."

"And even though she's a respected judge and an outspoken individual, you'll very rarely hear Carol put down another horse or trainer or rider. In this industry, if somebody gets hurt, we're the first to rally, but as a rule we can be pretty jealous people who don't give other riders or horses enough praise because we're jealous of them. There's a number of trainers Carol wouldn't send a horse to, but she doesn't go out and bad-mouth them."

Carol shares an affectionate respect for professionals who make a living with horses. Yet in characteristic style, she jokingly threatens to start breeding horse trainers to meet the demand for "one that can do it all." She's convinced they might even outsell her horses. "And if that works," she laughs, "I'd start breeding stall-muckers and truck drivers."

Short of breeding trainers, many have asked Carol to write an instruction book defining her program for raising champion horses and dogs. She dismisses that thought with a smile. "In all my years in this business, I've never followed a specific program because every animal needs an individual program. Each animal's care, handling and training must be determined by its behavior and they're all different," she explains.

"Intelligent breeding starts you down the road to success, but once the babies arrive, you must observe and evaluate each one daily to discover their natural propensities, preferences and personality."

"The more you watch the young ones, the more they reveal. Always let the animal tell you how it's most comfortable. Don't try to change him because everything will be easier for him if he's comfortable."

In the case of Rugged Lark, Carol noticed early on that he doesn't like pressure on his face or head. Since not having control of a stallion's head could prove dangerous down the line, others might have forced the issue and made the stud colt submit to constraints by using a snubbing post or lip chain until such time as he gave in—or blew up.

But Carol agrees with Will Rogers' warning, "When you give a lesson in meanness to a critter or a person, don't be surprised if they learn their lesson." Carol trains with trust and understanding, rather than intimidation or pain. As a result, she's shown halter horses extensively in world class competitions and has never used a lip chain because her stallions aren't permitted to require one.

Constraint never became an issue with Rugged Lark since Carol knew him well enough to realize he wasn't reacting out of dominance. He simply got anxious if his head was restricted...a natural, logical response for a prey animal. Rather than fight him on it, Carol showed him what she expected, then by adjusting, and literally giving Lark free rein, he learned to stand quietly with no restraints at all. This unusual treatment of a stallion set Rugged Lark up for many uniquely unfettered situations throughout his career. This remarkable aspect of his character would never have been developed, however, if Carol hadn't customized his training to accommodate that comfort point.

Bo-Bett's farrier, Craig Renwick, remembers a time when this training proved golden: "During breeding season, Carol was holding Rugged Lark in the barn's center aisle when someone called long distance. Carol said, 'I'm just going to leave him here and get the phone...you keep working.'"

"Then she dropped the lead line and left for the office while I continued working on Lark's hind foot. Suddenly the door beside me flew open and about ten Whippets exploded out. For a split second, I thought I was in big trouble holding the hind leg of a stallion, but Lark just stood there!"

"Now, I work on a lot of stallions, but that was a totally new experience for me. All the other stallions I do usually have a shank over their nose, in their mouth, or under their lip to keep them from biting or doing something quick. But Rugged Lark has always been a perfect gentleman. Whenever I work on him, he just lifts his feet for me—that's not usually how it goes for young stallions in training...."

A hands-on family operation such as Bo-Bett allows Carol to do much of the work herself. When she can't or doesn't have time to do something, she takes pains to find the right professional for the job. Where handling and training animals is concerned those referrals are critical.

Carol raises her horses and dogs with many of the same precepts with which she's raised her children, such as, understanding that like children, animals learn in their own way and in their own time.

Discovering Rugged Lark's versatile potential at the 1984 Congress brought with it the realization that future schooling would be with different trainers in a variety of disciplines. Carol knew she'd now be raising Lark by proxy and must be very careful to select trainers who supported her philosophy of love, trust and individualized training to develop happy, successful show animals.

"By the time Rugged Lark came around, I'd had a lot of experience with horses," notes Carol. "My biggest problem then became my age...a few bad falls had taken a toll. When it slowly sunk in that Rugged Lark was such a special animal, I knew I had to try to accommodate him with people who could do it right and make it pretty. He deserved a combination of respect and talent. But Lark's a hard horse to read unless you know him well, and mistakes with a horse like this would have to be kept to a minimum."

Now, Carol faced the daunting task of finding a whole string of trainers to entrust with her prized colt. Each trainer would be working on the canvas that was to become the competitive portrait of Rugged Lark. In order to succeed, they must share

©Reg Corkum

*"Now I work on a lot of stallions, but this horse is a gentleman,"*
*Bo-Bett's farrier, Craig Renwick*

*At the 1997 AQHA World Show in Oklahoma City, Carol expressed her appreciation to the following trainers for being such an important part of Rugged Lark's life. Left to Right are: Lynn Palm, Patty Shortino, Barbara Williams, Colleen McQuay, Bob Loomis, and Butch Campbell.*

the vision, the philosophy and the necessary techniques to collaborate on this equine work of art. Discord, ego and insensitivity would stand out on this mutual canvas in stark contrast to the integrated whole that Carol was working to design. Each collaborative team member would have to be chosen with tremendous care in order for this masterpiece to remain an inspired work.

Carol's anxiety at the delicate task ahead was heightened by the knowledge that Rugged Lark's home-schooling days were over. He'd progressed beyond the curriculum available at Bo-Bett. So now, like a devoted mother facing the prospect of sending her precocious child away to a series of boarding schools to study with various masters, Carol's mind filled with concern. How could she ever find all the proper trainers across so many disciplines who would bring Rugged Lark along the way she envisioned...and the way he deserved?

# Chapter Six
# In the Palm Of Her Hand
## "Winning Team Formula"

*A clean sweep for the Bo-Bett horses at the Florida Royal Two-Year-Old Snaffle Bit Western Pleasure Futurity. Shown winning first through third place are (left to right): Mike Corrington on Majestic Charity claiming second, Lynn Palm on Rugged Lark taking first, Jim Bryce on Foxy Majestic in third place, and owner, Carol Harris holding the ribbons.*

*(opposite page) Lark and Carol relax on the front porch of the Bo-Bett Farm office.*

It seems Mike Corrington paid an enormous personal price for that one extra spin at the 1984 Congress. Unable to face Carol, he packed up and left the show, Bo-Bett, and Florida without a word before she'd returned from Ohio. More than fifteen years later, even in light of Carol's assurances that the overspin redefined Rugged Lark's career for the better, Mike continues to kick himself. "You have no idea the hours I've spent thinkin' about that, but none of it changes.... The hardest part of that whole thing was I disappointed him."

The chain of events at the Congress left Carol with a maelstrom of training concerns. Lark's extraordinary multi-disciplinary potential made careful selection more vital than ever before, and now, with no resident trainer, Carol wasn't sure where to turn.

Although Carol had known Lynn Palm for a number of years as a school chum of her daughters, Lynn had only ridden a few of Carol's horses as a trainer. She'd done well with Rugged Lark, winning the

*Lark at home with Lynn in Bessemer, Michigan. This tropical baby found himself transported to the magnificent Michigan wilderness during snow season. It wasn't long before Carol received a call from Lynn saying, "Guess what Lark and I did today? We went for a sleigh ride!"*

1983 Florida Snaffle Bit Futurity on him as a two-year-old. (Actually, that Futurity was a clean sweep for Bo-Bett horses with Lynn and Lark taking first, Mike Corrington on Majestic Charity claiming second, and Jim Bryce on Foxy Majestic in third place.)

Seeing how well Rugged Lark and Lynn meshed when thrown into competitive deepwater with scant preparation during the Hunt Seat Futurity, Carol decided to bet on Lynn. It was obvious the partnership between Lark and Lynn had the requisite foundation of trust and love, and Carol's instincts told her this young trainer would build on Lark's inherent strengths. So when the 1984 Congress ended, Carol sent Lark home with Lynn to Bessemer, Michigan.

At thirty-two, Lynn Salvatori Palm had been training professionally for almost fifteen years, having learned her craft under the tutelage of Bobbi Steele, a highly respected trainer who was featured in a 1943 Life magazine article as being the first woman in the United States to ride Dressage. Trained by German riding masters of the Ringling Brothers Circus where she performed, Bobbi not only taught her students the European discipline of Dressage, she would not allow her beginning students the use of reins.

"Bobbi laid the basics for my career as a rider and trainer in Western Riding, Hunt Seat and Dressage," says Lynn. "It was a real priority for her that I learn to ride without my hands, so I learned to ride bridleless. This not only perfects the balanced form, it teaches the rider to communicate mainly from the waist down—with seat and legs—and minimally with hands. Bridleless riding forces you to feel and react to all the actions of your horse in order to maintain control. It's a huge confidence builder for a rider...plus, it's fun!"

As unusual as Miss Steele's method may have been, it taught the rider control from the leg up. When beginning riders are put on the back of a horse and given reins immediately, the horse suffers the consequence of inexperienced hands and uncoordinated balance. This also reinforces the natural inclination of a rider to hang on or grab for control with the reins. Learning to direct the horse with your leg, seat and weight first is more effective for the rider and kinder to the mount.

"Interestingly enough, Bobbi Steele was never a competitor," Lynn notes. "She was a performer who did fantastic exhibitions with horses all over the country from Madison Square Garden in New York to the American Royal in Kansas City."

Finding such an incredible mentor set young Lynn Salvatori on the path to horse heaven. By the time she was to graduate from high school her future was decided—professional horse trainer. Always a good student in school, by senior year she only needed two credits to graduate. At that time, colleges weren't offering degrees in horse training, so Lynn opted for practical experience spending part of her senior year in a special equestrian program in Ocala, Florida, schooling her horse, Mocha Dell, in bridleless routines.

That summer Lynn was hired by Frontier Town, a wild-west tourist attraction in upstate New York that contracted acts for its mock-rodeo events. Thus, while most of her friends were heading off to college, Lynn Salvatori and her loyal partner, Mocha Dell, were happily thrilling crowds by jumping bridleless...through flaming hoops of fire!

Although Lynn never put Rugged Lark through a ring of fire, she did introduce him to a great deal of new things—snow, for one. Suddenly, this tropical baby found himself transported to the magnificent Michigan wilderness during snow season. It wasn't long before Carol received a call from Lynn saying, "Guess what Lark and I did today? We went for a sleigh ride!" Carol was delighted by the mental image of her warm-blooded Florida-bred colt pulling a sleigh through drifts of snow.

"A very important training technique that I believe in, and follow religiously is, have fun with your horse," Lynn says emphatically. "Not just for the great times it allows, but for the more important sake of variety and expanding the horse's mind by introducing new situations and challenges. I don't care whether the animal's main training discipline is Western, Hunter, Jumper, Reining, Dressage, Amateur, Olympic or what.... Get out and have fun with that horse!"

"I not only broke Lark to pull the sleigh," Lynn recalls, "we went swimming in ponds, forded streams, did hill work; on the trail we'd practice upward and downward transitions, strengthen speed, slow the speed, work on straightness of lines.... The horse enjoys it because he's not having to do the same thing over and over, in the same spot, the same arena, the same routine.... Doing lots of different things keeps both horse and rider fresh and mentally open to new experiences. All that creates a healthy combination of conditioning work blended with technical training, which starts building a sound horse in mind and body that's going to last for a long time—and that's my goal."

"Regardless of what we did, Lark was always a good student," Lynn continues. "Now I've had horses that retain well and enjoy their work, but with Lark, many times I'd find myself stopping in amazement, saying, 'Lark, you shouldn't be doing this this well yet!' Then I'd have to reward him by putting him up. To this day I haven't had another horse that was that quick."

"And then, because he was so consistently correct, Rugged Lark taught me some very important lessons as a trainer. He proved to me that the better I rode, the better he'd do. If I was impeccably

*(opposite page)*
*Patty Shortino of Lutz, Florida*
*and Rugged Lark at*
*his first show over fences, which he won.*

balanced with my position, giving no interference whatsoever, he'd perform perfectly. And when I communicated with just the right amount of contact through my seat, legs or hands, he was always right there. Rugged Lark was so properly responsive when I asked correctly, that when things weren't progressing as expected it really made me stop and think. As a result I learned if he didn't respond to something I asked, the fault was probably with me."

"So now when something isn't going right, instead of trying to make it better by drilling or getting mad or frustrated, I stop and think about what's going on and look to myself for the solution to make it better. Rugged Lark taught me that," Lynn notes gratefully. "One other important lesson Lark taught me is you can't do your best without trust—you've got to trust your horse and he's got to trust you."

If Lynn couldn't resolve a training dilemma, she'd turn to Carol for advice, "When I'd have a little problem like a canter depart from a walk or a spin...whatever... the best advice Carol gave me was, 'Don't ride him. Take him out and just graze him, spend time with him.' I still don't know how or why that works, but in just doing that the problem invariably gets better!"

After his Michigan winter with Lynn, Lark returned to Florida to continue his expanded training program. This time, he was sent home with Patty Shortino in Lutz, Florida, to be started over fences. Patty's husband, Joey, had worked at Bo-Bett and was a Really Rugged fan who had shown many of Carol's colts before Rugged Lark was born, so Carol knew that Lark would be well-taken care of at the Shortino barn.

Like a proud schoolteacher, Patty recalls her student fondly, "Rugged Lark's a great individual with a great mind and great athletic ability, which is really rare in one horse. He was so accepting of everything, no matter what it was you wanted to try to do, he always tried to help out."

One episode stands out for her: "We took Lark to a local hunter schooling show and he won. Some of the hunter people there asked about breeding to him because they thought he was cute and he jumped so well. So Joey starts telling them about how Lark won the Florida Snaffle Bit Futurity, the Reining Pre-Futurity in Louisville, and the Hunt Seat Futurity at the Congress.... Hearing that, one woman asked, 'Wow! How old is he?'

"Joey says, 'Three.'"

"Well, her jaw dropped in astonishment, 'That horse is only three and he's won all that? How could a three year old do all that?'"

Patty did a great job with Lark, for in January of 1985 he won two championships over fences at the Florida Gold Coast Circuit.

Following his time with the Shortinos, Lark moved on to Barbara Williams in North Carolina, who brushed up and added to his reining skills. She qualified him for the World Show in Reining while Lynn qualified him in Hunt Seat, Driving and Western Riding. Although Carol and Lynn had the Superhorse competition in the back of their minds, it was never their main focus. They simply worked toward having Lark do his best in each of his individual events, then what was meant to be would happen.

As Lynn recalls, "It was so wonderful working with Carol because as a breeder, owner and a horseman she's always maintained, 'Just do your best job, it can't always be perfect and if something

*January of 1985 - Rugged Lark and Lynn Palm
won two championships in the over-fences classes at the Florida Gold Coast Circuit.
Pictured with Lynn are owner Carol Harris and to her right Mary Kaye Striegel.*

doesn't go right, it's okay—that's part of horses—then we just move on and do better next time. But keep me informed...don't paint a rosy picture that everything's going great if it's not.'"

"So there was always a real good rapport that way, and as a result, no real stresses ever built up. Some owners demand, 'You gotta win! This is a stud, the only way he's gonna do well is if he wins.' Carol never had that attitude. As a younger trainer, it was remarkably good and very special for me to have her kind of generous support."

"So we just aimed for doing well in all our events and Rugged Lark won the All Around Championship at the 1985 Congress," reports Lynn, who was particularly thrilled by that win for she had put much of it together with Rugged Lark: finishing his Driving style, then showing him beautifully in Driving, Western and Hunt Seat events.

Only a few weeks later they were off to the World Show in Oklahoma City. Not as large as the Congress, the World Show's prestige is based on the fact that its events are limited to contests between the top contenders in each event. All horses must earn the right to compete at the World Show by accumulating qualifying points at competitions throughout the year. Thus a win at the World Show represents a singular triumph over the cream of the competitive crop. Additionally, the World Show is the arena for that most coveted Quarter Horse title: Superhorse!

*Rugged Lark is pictured winning the All Around with Chris Wirtzberger at The 1985 All American Quarter Horse Congress.*

Instituted in 1978, this annual award honors the horse with the greatest number of points garnered across three or more World Show events. Similar to an athlete winning the Pentathlon at the Olympics, the Superhorse award identifies the royalty of competitively versatile Quarter Horses.

Walter Hughes, a well-respected horseman from Maryland, recalls judging at the 1985 World Show, "Rugged Lark had qualified in seven different events...both Western and English. It seemed to me every time I went to judge an event, here comes this big, pretty, bay stud horse again—we sure saw a lot of him that week! Now any horse that can qualify for the World Show in that many different events is special.... But Rugged Lark had the ability to be competitive in every event in which he showed! He had such a wonderful mind he was able to handle it all—he just looked like the kind of horse that whatever was asked of him, he very seldom, if ever, said, 'No.'"

Barbara Williams qualified Rugged Lark in Reining for the World Show, then claimed third place in Junior Reining with him. Lynn Palm qualified Rugged Lark in all his other events, then guided him to

Rugged 61 Lark

the World Championship in Pleasure Driving and to a list of fifth places in Junior Working Hunter, Junior Hunter Hack, Junior Trail and Junior Hunter Under Saddle. When the World Show points were finally tallied, Rugged Lark's totalled forty-two! Carol had known all along that this plain bay colt was a special horse, and now it was officially confirmed that he was, in fact, a Superhorse!

As cumulative high-point competitor at the World Show, the Superhorse is recognized as the ultimate performance horse. The fact that Lark won the title in such a variety of events under both Western and English tack underscored his exceptional versatility as well.

Carol and Lynn were ecstatic with the win. Their faith in Lark was growing stronger and they began laying plans for an even brighter future for this talented young Superhorse.

The next year brought another brilliant bit of plumage to Rugged Lark's cap when he was declared the 1986 High Point Driving Stallion, then became the 1986 Versatility Champion at the All American Quarter Horse Congress. Again, Lynn's multifaceted training program met the test and turned out a winner.

But that year, Rugged Lark was unable to defend his Superhorse title since he was ineligible to participate in the World Show. Carol's critical eye and disciplined focus made her a highly valued judge and the AQHA Judges Committee had invited Carol to judge the 1986 World Show. To eliminate any chance of favoritism or conflict of interest in judging, horses owned by judges are not allowed to compete.

In spite of the fact that the invitation eliminated Rugged Lark from World Show competition, Carol was excited and honored to be asked and took her judging jobs seriously—as the following

*Barbara Williams is pictured on her way to qualifying Rugged Lark in Reining for the AQHA World Show.*

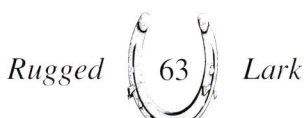

*Lynn Palm guides Rugged Lark to the 1985 AQHA World Championship in Pleasure Driving.*

story illustrates:

"About fifteen years ago," reports Keith Bradley, "I was announcing while Carol was judging Cutting at the All American Quarter Horse Congress. At that time judges sat in chairs on flat-bed wagons wheeled in for each event. While one Cutting horse was working a cow, a rogue steer broke out of the herd and jumped up on Carol's wagon, clambering to within a few feet of her. He stood there blowin' but Carol didn't bat an eye—she was concentrating on that Cutter!"

"That old steer watched the cutting with Carol for a while, then finally jumped off...photographer Harold Campton caught it all on film."

"I remember wondering, 'Now how many people could do that?' Most would have got flustered with a steer up there and stopped the action, saying, 'Hey, wait a minute, I've got to get rid of this thing!' But it didn't bother Carol at all...she just sat there and marked her card!"

With that kind of dedication it's no wonder she was well-respected as a judge!

Nineteen eighty-seven brought a new shot at World Show events. This time trainer Bob Loomis was in charge of Lark's reining work, so Lark went to Bob's ranch in Marietta, Oklahoma. A renowned horseman, Bob has won the National Reining Futurity six times and the World Reining Championship nine times, as well as countless World Championships in both Working Cow and Western Riding.

Even with all Bob's years of riding, training and showing, however, Rugged Lark proved to be a unique experience. Lark had so much training on him in so many different disciplines, was so naturally responsive and knew such a variety of cues, that he was a complex and challenging ride.

*1985 Super Horse Rugged Lark celebrates his win with owner, Carol Harris, and riders, Lynn Palm and Barbara Williams.*

Rugged 64 Lark

*Lark and Carol pick up the awards for the Superhorse win which included a check for $10,000.*

*Rugged Lark is named the
1986 All American Quarter Horse Congress Versatility Champion.
Lark is surrounded by his friends and family.
Ted McLelland is pictured awarding the trophy saddles.*

Carol still laughs about the time she overheard Bob giving his assistant, Dean Latimer, last-minute instructions when Dean was to ride Lark in a qualifying show. Warning him about Lark's many 'buttons' and ultra-fine tuning, Bob cautioned, "As you come toward the center, don't you even dare fart or he'll change leads on ya'!"

But what Bob Loomis remembers most about Lark's time at his ranch was the loving bond his young daughter developed with the stallion, "Bobbi Jo was about eleven then and spent a lot of time in the barn with me. She was in the stall playin' with that horse all the time he was here. She just was always fiddling with him...pettin' on him, rubbin' him down—I even caught her under him currying his stomach! But I knew she was perfectly safe with Lark. That horse has got a very special attitude...he's a very, very safe horse. You'd never have to worry about him ever hurting anybody."

"I'd school Rugged Lark each day and when I was done riding, Bobbie Jo'd take him out bareback with just a halter and lead rope and ride him around the big hayfield...just walking him to cool him out; then she'd stop and let him eat grass.... Pretty soon the line would be layin' in the dirt and she'd be asleep

(top photo) Larry Sullivant, Carol Harris, & Kenneth Jackson judging a horse show.

(bottom photo) Bob Loomis and daughter, Bobbi Jo

on his back...she'd fall fast asleep on his back while he was eating grass out there."

"I've only been around two stallions like that in my life, him and Topsail Whiz are the only two stallions I've known that were just plain sweet. Rugged Lark is happiest when you're doin' something with him—he just loves being with people."

Bob Loomis easily qualified Lark for Reining at the World Show and Lynn was busy qualifying him once again in Driving, Western Riding, Trail, and three Hunt Seat events. Little did they realize what was in store when they all convened in Oklahoma City for the 1987 World Show....

Shortly after settling in at the Show, Lynn climbed onto a stool to braid the mane of a rather tall hunter when the horse suddenly swung its head, knocking her clear across the aisle. She hit the opposite wall, bounced against a tack trunk and landed on the cement floor—hard! Luckily no bones were broken, but it felt like every muscle and ligament in her body had been twisted and tied.

Valiantly she reported for the first of her events with Rugged Lark, Western Riding, where they did well enough to claim second place.

Then it was Bob Loomis's turn with Lark in the Senior Reining competition where they took a fourth.

Now, Lynn faced the Senior Hunter Hack event. Despite her condition, she convinced Carol that working would help limber her muscles, then proceeded to ride Lark to the Reserve World Championship in that event! But by now, her bruised muscles had stiffened so that even a slight movement made her groan. How could

Rugged 67 Lark

(top photo) Colleen McQuay

(bottom photo) Joe Edge

she continue competing at a World Show level if she couldn't move?

A brief medical check reconfirmed no breaks, but the only remedy the doctor offered was time—which she didn't have. To ease the worst of the soreness, he gave her a couple of pain pills. As the medication took hold, Lynn was able to move more freely and soon felt like she could handle the next class—thankfully it was the Trail event. Lynn and Lark had already accumulated enough points throughout the year to earn the Superior Trail Horse award, so of all the events, this would be one of their most confident contests.

Gamely, Lynn hauled herself into the saddle and headed into the arena. The two walked, jogged and loped, opened gates, made it around difficult obstacles, and backed beautifully. Then Lynn expertly side-passed Lark along a low rail—straight and smooth and correct.... By this time Lynn was feeling no pain—literally and figuratively—but the pills distorted her judgement and she turned Lark too soon...before he'd reached the end of the pole. As a result of the premature cue, Lark's leg knocked the pole off it's support and their promising score tumbled down along with the rail.

Could the rest of Rugged Lark's combined events counter this lowered score? Only time would tell, but at that point Carol was not focused on the Superhorse title. She was marveling at the laudable courage and competence Lynn was displaying under the circumstances.

Looking ahead to the remaining events, Lynn felt she could still handle the Pleasure Driving and Hunter Under Saddle competitions—without medication this time! However, she realistically admitted that she might not be up to the jumping required in the Working Hunter event.

After discussions with Carol, they both agreed another rider should show Lark in Senior Working Hunter. But where to find someone at the last minute capable of eliciting a performance worthy of defending the Superhorse title? Lynn reminded Carol that Colleen McQuay had recently been schooling Rugged Lark over fences.... Thankfully, Colleen stepped up to this eleventh-hour challenge and secured a third in that event.

As Colleen recalls, "Riding Rugged Lark was like flying a 747—you'd better make sure you're touching the right button! Not because he'd do anything wrong, he just might do an extra maneuver or change something simply because he was trying to please by responding to all the buttons. The rider has to be able to synchronize all the cues correctly."

"He was one of the first horses I'd trained that had a high education to which I was adding more," Colleen continues, "so he taught me a lot about the sensitivity of horses, how to separate instructions and be patient and let the horse help me teach it. Some trainers have one system and the horse has to use their system. Because I had so much respect for Rugged Lark, I allowed him to teach me as we were going along. I would try some of my usual techniques, and since he was easy to read, I could see which exercises helped and which were hard for him. Thus, it was easy for him to teach me 'his system'—those things that benefitted him. Ever since then, I've learned that every horse has something to teach you."

"It is very difficult for a horse to go from one trainer to the next, to the next," Colleen notes, "I've seen resulting difficulties in many horses...especially with a stallion! But I had no problem with Rugged Lark—he was easy to bond with, easy to read, very smooth to ride, easy to jump...and easy to have confidence in because he's so honest. He is a very, very, honest horse. And because he has such a big heart and is not fearful, you knew that unless you, the rider, made a mistake, you'd be able to do what you needed to do. Lark was happy in his job,

*Although very ill at the time, Carol's friend, Babe Ruth, made it to her wedding to Bill Winans in 1945.*

and always tried to be your partner. That's an extremely rewarding situation—it's a lot more comfortable to be in a situation where you can count on a partner instead of someone who's making you carry the whole load! I knew if I was on target, he'd be right there with me. The high-tech level of winning or not was in the test of whether I was sensitive enough to synchronize all his education and make it work...it was pretty exciting!"

With the last minute Senior Working Hunter crisis so well-resolved, Carol was able to relax and enjoy some World Show camaraderie with her buddy, Sue Page. Outside one of the arena's, a horseman by the name of Joe Edge had drawn a line in the dirt and was pitching quarters with a few cowboys.

*(top photo)*
*Carol with friend, Babe Ruth,
and a neighbor boy,
fishing together at Little Flat Brook.*

*(opposite page)*
*(top photo)*
*Rugged Lark collects his check for winning
the 1987 Super Horse Award. This was his second win.*

*(bottom photo)*
*Mike Corrington returns, with Lynn and Carol,
to celebrate Lark's milestone win.*

As Sue reports, "Joe's a very influential man who, like Carol, is a bit outrageous and enjoys pullin' pranks. He knew Carol was always up for fun and would do most anything—she's sort of the Carol Burnett of the horse industry—a crazy, funny nut who loves people. So Joe challenged her to pitch for a dollar bet. Carol says, 'Nah, I can't do that...I couldn't!'"

"But Joe egged her on, 'Aw, c'mon Carol, just give it a try....'"

"So she takes the quarter and starts acting real silly—crouching down low, then raising her butt high in the air, wigglin' it around and kinda stiff-arms the quarter.... Like iron shot to a magnet, that coin landed right on the line!"

"Then Joe throws his quarter and it ends up about three inches off."

"Well, okay, that was luck...so they keep going.... She'd miss some and he'd miss some, but Joe kept upping the stakes again and again until they had a pretty good-sized little wager going."

"That's when Carol says, 'I'm out. Hey, I'm not that good.'"

"But Joe wouldn't let her quit, 'Now come on Carol, just one more throw....'"

"'Oh, all right,' Carol says, sounding doubtful and a bit perturbed as she bends down, does her little butt-wavin' antics, and flips the coin in a high, spinning arc that drops flat on the line once again!"

"Joe paid up and walked off shaking his head at such incredible beginner's luck."

"I looked at Carol and asked, 'Now where'd you learn to do that?'"

"'Babe Ruth,' she replied as she palmed her winnings."

"'Babe Ruth! What do you mean?'"

Rugged 71 Lark

"Carol grinned as she explained that Babe Ruth had been a great friend of her father's and whenever he had the time, Babe would join her family at their home in Hainesville, New Jersey. Babe loved to fish the Little Flat Brook that ran through the property, but was too tender-hearted to bait a worm or pull the hook out of a trout's mouth...so that became Carol's job. In return for her helping him with that, he taught her how to skip stones across the pond, throw balls...and pitch quarters."

It seems Carol was born with a knack for finding the best of trainers!

Through the years Carol has often used her Babe Ruth pitching talent in training young horses to come to the pasture gate when she calls. If they don't start over right away, she'll pitch a pebble at their rump to cue them to the command...that practice has developed pretty dependable "pitch-manship"!

A few years back, Carol's daughter, Allison, found an old photo of Babe and Carol fishing together at Little Flat Brook and had it beautifully framed as a surprise for Carol—a truly charming portrait of two American pitching champions.

After her victory at the quarter pitchin' event, Carol turned her attention back to the contest at hand. In addition to the events mentioned above, Lynn and Lark managed to take Reserve World Champion Pleasure Driving and World Champion Hunter Under Saddle! Carol was thrilled, but still didn't know if Lark had enough points to top this year's tough competition for Superhorse.

As Carol walked over to the office with Lynn and Sue to check the standings, she thought about how lucky she was to have found so many able, appreciative trainers for Lark. Even though she oftentimes had to relinquish Lark's care and training to others, Carol always worked closely with those select professionals—especially Lynn Palm—that way she kept Rugged Lark's training in the palm of her hand. Such teamwork was fun for all concerned and Lark flourished in the process, obviously enjoying the many different tasks he was asked to do.

Carol could scarcely contain her excitement when the tally showed that this exceptional team effort just made Quarter Horse history. Rugged Lark's fifty-one points not only smashed his 1985 Superhorse score, it made him the first ever two-time Superhorse!

Letting out a victory whoop, Carol left to find Colleen and Bob to tell them the good news, then rushed back to the barn area to help Lynn prepare Lark for the awards ceremony.

Often described as tough but fair, Carol is widely respected for her knowledge, ability and judgement, but she's loved for her generous heart, open mind and outrageous sense of fun. A consummate entertainer, she's constantly on the lookout for new ideas and novel surprises. With Rugged Lark taking his second Superhorse title, she and Lynn wanted to spark the awards ceremony by doing "something different".

That night the stands were packed with spectators watching the final Working Cow and Junior Cutting events. As those contests were won and the championships awarded, the crowd's attention focused on the title of Superhorse.

Finally, the moment of anticipation arrived... The buzz of the crowd dropped to a soft murmur as the arena lights dimmed and the air filled with the pronouncement: "The winner of the 1987 Superhorse Title is Rugged Lark!"

A trio of spotlights swept across the empty ring to the in-gate where Lynn and Lark were suddenly awash in light and applause as they trotted proudly into the arena. Simultaneously, the huge video monitors suspended above came to life showing clips of Rugged Lark competing in his six winning events.

Rugged Lark was resplendent with his dark coat brushed to the rich glow of burnished bronze setting off the vibrant floral neck-ring he'd received for his Hunter Under Saddle World Championship. All eyes followed the pair to the awards area. Only then did it begin to dawn on the spectators that this

*Lynn Palm rides Lark bridleless to accept the 1987 Superhorse Award.*

Superhorse was wearing no bridle!

After the Superhorse Award presentation, to a chorus of cheers, the champions trotted to the center of the arena. Then Lynn spun Lark left, stopped clean and spun him to the right—with no reins, no headstall, no bit! The crowd went nuts!

Seeing that Lark wasn't bothered by the pandemonium, Lynn decided to go for it.... Nudging him into a lope, they circled the arena with Lark skipping rhythmically, changing leads every few strides to Lynn's invisible cues. As they approached the outgate, Lynn raised both arms high above her head, and waving like a joyous rodeo queen, saluted the thousands of charged fans who'd jumped to their feet in excitement as she and Rugged Lark gave them the most memorable victory lap in the history of Superhorse competition.

That spontaneous spark of bridleless riding at the 1987 World Show not only thrilled those Superhorse fans, it set the legend of Rugged Lark afire!

# Pedigree of Rugged Lark

```
                                                                    ┌─ Sting (TB) ──────────┬─ Spur (TB)
                                            ┌─ Questionnaire (TB) ──┤                        └─ Gnat (TB)
                                            │                       └─ Miss Puzzle (TB) ────┬─ Disguise (TB)
                         ┌─ FREE FOR ALL (TB) SW                                             └─ Ruby Nethersole (TB)
                         │  $111,225.    6 wins                     ┌─ *Chicle (TB) ────────┬─ =Spearmint (TB)
                         │  6 wins, from 7 starts, at 2 and 3.      │                        └─ Lady Hamburg 2nd (T
                         │  won: Arlington Futurity, Washington ────┤
                         │  Park Futurity, Hyde Park S.             │                       ┌─ Whisk Broom 2nd (TB)
                         │                   foal of 1942           └─ Panasette (TB) ──────┤
     ┌─ ROUGH'N TUMBLE (TB) SW  Panay (TB)                                                   └─ Panasine (TB)
     │   $126,980.   4 wins                                         ┌─ *Teddy (TB) ─────────┬─ =Ajax (TB)
     │   won: Santa Anita Derby, Primer Stakes                      │                        └─ =Rondeau (TB)
     │            foal of 1948                ┌─ *Bull Dog (TB) ────┤
     │                                        │                    └─ =Plucky Liege (TB) ──┬─ =Spearmint (TB)
     │                         ┌─ ROUSED (TB) ┤                                             └─ =Concertina (TB)
     │                         │  unplaced    │                                             ┌─ Whisk Broom 2nd (TB)
     │                         │  foal of 1943│                    ┌─ Upset (TB) ──────────┤
     │                         │              └─ Rude Awakening (TB)                        └─ Pankhurst (TB)
     │                         │                                   └─ Cushion (TB) ────────┬─ Nonpareil (TB)
REALLY RUGGED (TB)                                                                           └─ Hassock (TB)
$16,000.   3 wins                                                   ┌─ *Challenger 2nd (TB)─┬─ =John O' Gaunt (TB)
foal of 1960                                                        │                        └─ =Canterbury Pilgrim (
                         ┌─ ERRARD (TB) SW  ───┬─ Ruddy Light (TB) ─┤                       ┌─ =Great Sport (TB)
                         │  $36,630.   6 wins │                    └─ *Honeywood (TB) ─────┤
                         │  won: Prairie State S., Crete H.                                  └─ =Flash Of Steel (TB)
                         │  2nd: Joliet S.; 3rd: Cowdin S.,                                  ┌─ =Polymelus (TB)
                         │  Futurity S., Washington Park Fut.       ┌─ Sweep (TB) ──────────┤
     │                   │                 foal of 1942             │                        └─ =Honeybird (TB)
     │                   │                     └─ Washoe Belle (TB)─┤
     └─ RUDDY BELLE (TB)                                            └─ Grace Commoner (TB) ─┬─ *Teddy (TB)
        $17,165.   7 wins                                                                    └─ =Plucky Liege (TB)
        foal of 1949                          ┌─ Sir Damion (TB) ───┬─ *Sir Gallahad 3rd (TB)┬─ *Omar Khayyam (TB)
                         └─ HARRIET'S KID (TB)│                     └─ Ommiad (TB) ─────────┬─ *Sunstep (TB)
                            $1,650.  placed  │                                               └─ *North Star 3rd (TB)
                            foal of 1944      │                    ┌─ Bubbling Over (TB) ──┬─ Beaming Beauty (TB)
                                              └─ Liz F. (TB) ──────┤
                                                                   └─ Weno (TB) ───────────┬─ Whisk Broom 2nd (TB)
                                                                                            └─ Rosie O'grady (TB)
```

*1985 AQHA World Show Superhorse*
*1987 AQHA World Show Superhorse*
*Twice AQHA World Champion Performance Horse*
*Three-time AQHA High Point Performance Horse*

**RUGGED LARK**

# Pedigree Chart

**AQHA #2,086,479    1981 bay stallion**
Breeder: Teresa Striegel, Reddick FL
Owner: Carol A. Harris, Bo-Bett Farm
Reddick, FL

## LEOLARK
*Show ROM*
*AQHA Champion*

### LEMAC -A-
$402.    4 racing points
Breeder: Bud Warren
Perry, OK

- **Leo**
  - Joe Reed II
    - Joe Reed P-3
    - Nellene
  - Little Fanny
    - Joe Reed P-3
    - Fanny Ashwell
- **Sorrel Sue**
  - King P-234
    - Zantanon
    - Jabalina
  - Tommy King mare
    - Tommy King
    - --

### TALLULAH
#93,798    1959 chestnut
Breeder: Skylark Farms
Concord, CA
*1959 AQHA High Point Working Cowhorse Mare*

- **King Bob**
  - Brown Bob
    - Snooper
    - by/ Harmon Baker Jr
  - Queen Ann
    - King P-234
    - Holland mare
- **Daisy K**
  - Copper
    - Tom Benear
    - May Troutman
  - Scar Face
    - Golden Bear (TB)
    - Georgia

## ALISA LARK
#601,945    1969 brown
Breeder: Skylark Farms
Galt, CA
*AQHA Champion*
*1978 AJQHA World Champion Hunter Under Saddle*
*1978 AJQHA World Champion Hunt Seat Equitation*

### PELICAN -AAA-
#30,381    1949 chestnut
Breeder: Lou Kosloff
Encino, CA
*1947 Champion Qtr Running Stallion*

- **Joe Hancock Jr**
  - Joe Hancock
    - John Wilkens
    - unknown
  - Burnett mare
    - --
    - --
- **Covella (TB)**
  - Coventry (TB)
    - *Negofol (TB)
    - Sun Queen (TB)
  - Sonora (TB)
    - *Light Brigade (TB)
    - Ilma (TB)

### ALISO GILL 3
#55,092    1944 chestnut
Breeder: J. W. Culbertson
Albuquerque, NM
*A Leading Dam of AQHA Champions*

- **Snicker**
  - John Gaston
    - Nowata Star
    - Chouteau
  - Fleet
    - Sappho / Brown King
    - --

### SNICKER GIRL
#130,141    1958 brown
Breeder: Will Gill and Sons
Madera, CA

- **Okie Girl**
  - Joe Tom
    - Joe Hancock
    - Thoroughbred mare
  - Miss Tommy 99
    - Tom (Scooter)
    - riding type mare

#39,321    1950 brown
Breeder: W. W. Cecil Jr.
Winters, CA

---

## PREMIER PEDIGREES

AQHA • NCHA • Thoroughbred • Pedigrees & Catalogs

P.O. Box 148
Wamego, KS 66547    FAX: (913) 456-9620

Data provided by Premier Pedigrees is generally accurate, but occasionally errors and omissions occur as a result of incorrect data received from others, mistakes in processing and other causes. Premier Pedigrees disclaims responsibility for the consequences, if any, of such errors, but would appreciate their being called to it's attention.

| ROM | Register of Merit | SI | Speed Index | TB | Thoroughbred | NTR | New Track Record |
|-----|-------------------|----|-----|----|----|----|----|
| QH | Quarter Horse | SW | Stakes Winner | * | Imported TB | ETR | Equalled Track Record |

# Chapter Seven
# Six Year-Old Retiree
## "Retired and Still Winning"

Nineteen eighty-seven was truly a triumphant year for Rugged Lark. In addition to his Reserve and World Championships and the unprecedented Superhorse repeat, he was awarded AQHA awards for Superior Trail Horse, High Point Hunter Hack Stallion and High-Point Working Hunter Stallion, as well as being elected to the Florida Quarter Horse Hall of Fame. Considering the meteoric speed with which Lark's broad career had reached historic heights, Carol questioned where he could go from here.

After all, Lark was only six years-old—just entering his mature prime—but in light of what he'd accomplished, Carol saw no real benefit in campaigning him any further. Road trips and competitions open the door to risk of accident, stress and injury. In addition, word had gotten back to Carol through friends that Lark's seemingly invincible proficiency was beginning to foster frustration and resentment in a few show circles—especially the Hunter arena.

As news of Rugged Lark's most recent Hunt Seat victories circulated, some competitors were overheard saying, "That damn 'Poco-Bueno-with-braids' beat us again!" Referring to the popular, successful Quarter Horse sire of years past whose get won so consistently in Halter and Cutting classes that if your horse didn't have 'Poco' in it's name you'd think twice about entering.

At 15:2 1/2 hands, Rugged Lark is small compared to the majority of Hunt Seat

*(top photo) Lynn Palm and Rugged Lark on their way to earning his Superior in Trail.*

*(bottom photo) Rugged Lark, the "Poco-Bueno-with-braids"*

# American Quarter Horse Association

January 20, 1988

Carol A. Harris Parker
Rt 1 Box 369
Reddick, FL 32686

Dear Carol:

It is my pleasure to enclose the AQHA Superior Trail Horse certificate on your outstanding horse, RUGGED LARK, #2,086,479.

He has earned this award by winning at least fifty points in Trail.

Our congratulations and best wishes for continued success.

                Very truly yours,

                AMERICAN QUARTER HORSE ASSOCIATION


                Dan Delaney
                Director of Shows and Youth Activities

DD/dab
enc.

horses which tend to be more thoroughbred-y in height. However, in spite of his relatively small stature, which might have been a disadvantage, like Poco Bueno, he won consistently. Thus the nickname probably grew out of a mix of respect, envy and perhaps just a touch of resentment.

Even with her legendary sense of humor, Carol found it hard to laugh at such remarks. She was disturbed at the thought that there might be any rancor building up against Rugged Lark's success. She loves this horse dearly—he is so good and kind—she wants everyone to love him. Even in jest, that kind of bitter joke can spur unhealthy jealousies, and with such high stakes in competition, it only takes one nut trying to eliminate a roadblock to the top...as the Striegel's could attest. Lynn Palm had also had a frightening experience when one of her top horses had acid thrown on its back! Thankfully, there was no permanent damage, but these incidents serve as a flashing warning that high-profile competitors can become targets for a warped mind.

Since young Rugged Lark had climbed the highest peaks in the industry so rapidly, establishing both a historic record and a superlative reputation, there weren't many competitive challenges ahead. So, after his second Superhorse win, Carol retired Lark from competition in 1987.

Retired, but definitely not forgotten. Such an exceptional equine athlete remains indelibly etched in the hearts and minds of true horsemen. Lark's awe-inspiring record and magical performances kept people talking and thinking...wondering how does he do it? What makes this horse so uniquely captivating, versatile and successful?

Trainer Butch Campbell believes Rugged Lark's natural action underlies his ability to excel at both Hunt Seat and Western disciplines, "Rugged Lark is slow legged for Western, yet he has a great stride for Hunt Seat, so he can go either way and excel at both. When he strides out, he doesn't move his body to cover ground, his legs just sweep the ground efficiently..."

Professional breeder and trainer, Don

*(top photo)*
*Carol and Trainer Butch Campbell*

*(bottom photo)*
*Dr. G. Marvin Beeman*

# BO-BETT FARM

Route #1, Box 369
Reddick, Florida 32686

Farm (904)
(904)

January 12, 1988

Ms. Juli J. Klee
Levi Strauss & Co.
Levi's Plaza
P.O. Box 7215
San Francisco, CA  94120

Dear Julie:

I want to thank you for the very generous check that you gave to the American Quarter Horse Association for the Levi's Superhorse Award.

We were absolutely thrilled to win it with our six-year old Stallion, Rugged Lark.

Everybody at Bo-Bett Farm wears Levis, and you can be sure we are going to keep wearing them.

If you are ever in Florida, we would love to introduce you to Rugged Lark and to show you around Ocala.

Many thanks again to everyone at Levi Strauss and Co.  Best wishes to all of you for 1988.

Sincerely,

BO-BETT FARM

Carol A. Harris Parker

cc Don Treadway

McDuffee feels it goes beyond movement, to motivation and management, "I've been associated with Rugged Lark before he was even born and I've watched him through every phase of his career. Just a few months ago, I saw a routine they did with him here in Ocala, Florida, and as many times as I've seen Lark, it still gives me goosebumps to watch him work. To watch his expression, to see what this horse is capable of doing and how effortlessly he does it. To have a horse that wants to perform for somebody like that is remarkable.... It takes a good horse and a great owner to get that out of an animal."

Even the AQHA sought answers by making a video of Rugged Lark to study and illustrate effective conformation under the guidance of specialist, Dr. G. Marvin Beeman. An equine practitioner who's been involved with the AQHA veterinary seminars on conformation as an instructor and lecturer since 1970, Dr. Beeman reports, "My passion, as well as my profession, has been the evaluation of the horse's structure in relationship of form to function, so I've spent a great deal of time discussing and thinking about conformation."

*(bottom photo) An advertisement for the Breyer Horse Model of Rugged Lark*

"There are three basic reasons why I appreciate Rugged Lark as much as I do. One: he's extremely well-balanced, he's got a beautiful head and his athletic ability is exemplified by his wonderful conformation. But conformation's not the only factor that makes horses do what they do, there are several intrinsic factors that also have to work—all the structures and systems that combine to make their form relate to function. This includes the musculo-skeletal system, nervous system, cardiovascular system, respiratory system and, of course, the digestive system."

"Another factor that certainly influences a horse is his ability to be trained and the horse's ability to accept what man asks him to do. Then, of course, his training.... Lynn Palm was riding Rugged Lark every time I saw him and I have a tremendous amount of respect for her, but she also had a wonderful student in Rugged Lark."

"The third aspect is hard to define—it's what horsemen call 'heart' or 'try'. As a veterinarian I look at it from the standpoint of his physical heart coupled with his ability to perform whenever he's asked to."

"When you combine conformation, performance and heart you've got the kind of horse that every horseman should step back and study very, very closely because they only come around once in a great while. Secretariat was a very similar kind of horse. He had the conformation, the ability to perform, and a personality that was unique."

"We must stand back and think about these horses in depth—not just a conversation like, 'Oh, yes, he's a beautiful horse, I really like him....' There's much more to it than we are even able to articulate in many cases. It's not just how well his shoulder is angled and how well his arm's attached...it's the entire package: his size, his width, his length...all of that coupled with such efficiently functioning physical systems is what makes a horse like Rugged Lark so spectacular."

Evidently others agreed with Dr. Beeman's assessment, for in 1989, Bo-Bett Farm's model horse also became a popular, collectible Breyer horse model.

Despite Rugged Lark's career triumphs and bustling breeding schedule, by the end of the 1980's not everything at Bo-Bett was happily on track. Carol's nearly twelve-year marriage was disintegrating. Her husband had left town and it appeared her third marriage would end much the way her second had. A nasty divorce is the last thing anyone needs at any time. At this time, Carol endured lost sleep, lost trust, and a lost sense of security. But worst of all, since he was one of the marital assets, she also faced the real possibility of losing Rugged Lark. Now Carol faced a tough fight, but she was determined to fight—for her farm, her horses and her financial life.

During the ordeal of an entire year of legal investigations, depositions, meetings, financial reviews and hearings, Carol relied on humor to renew her spirit and maintain her equilibrium. Jokes flew around the office as everyone tried to think up names for the current foal crop to reflect the sorry legal focus that had descended on Bo-Bett.

The final divorce decree left her reeling. Although she was eternally grateful that she would be able to keep Rugged Lark, her legal bills necessitated a huge disposition sale of horses and foals.

By the time the sale came around, the pain was eased a bit since Carol couldn't help but smile as the auctioneer announced each of the sale's yearlings: Lark's Indiscretion, Lark's Sweet Affair, Lark's Expert Witness, Lark's Deposition, Lark's First Appeal, Lark's Appraisal, Lark's Joint Account, Lark's Bank Note, Lark's Trust Fund, Lark's Cashier Check, Lark's Stop Payment, Lark's Day In Court, Lark's Hanky Panky, and Joan of Lark.

In the end, Carol's most heartfelt loss was not her husband; it was an exceptional son of Rugged Lark by the name of Regal Lark and a favorite young roping mare, Joyful Lark. When these two favorites left Bo-Bett Farm, Carol never looked back except for the occasional twinges of loss she felt whenever she heard of or watched Regal Lark's accomplishments. The young stallion was indeed a standout and was thankfully brought along by good trainers. At the World Show in 1993, Regal Lark missed the Superhorse title by only a single point, claiming the Reserve Superhorse crown.

"I survived that ordeal thanks to my friends who kept me laughing when I might have been crying," says Carol. "I was able to screw my head on tighter and return to a much better life."

With the divorce and near-dispersal sale behind her, there was one last ritual Carol needed to perform before her catharsis was complete. As her final symbolic act of divorce, Carol took a sheet of circular stickers, drew heavy diagonal bar sinisters through them and placed one carefully over her ex's face in each of the family and show-awards photographs in which he was included.

"I've never thrown away any of my precious pictures to erase memories," says Carol. "I simply take undesirable folks out of them by covering their face with 'personal prohibition stickers' as a reminder of what I shouldn't have done."

In surveying the impressive Bo-Bett photo gallery, a number of these are evident and you can't help but laugh at these funny, home-made, cathartic ex-husband out-takes.

The decade of the 1990's ushered in a new era for Rugged Lark. Although retired from competition, Lark continued gaining renown as an exceptional sire. In 1991, he became the first Superhorse in history to sire a Superhorse when his 1987 colt, The Lark Ascending, was proclaimed World Champion

*(top photo)*
*Regal Lark, owned by Joan Cain and R. Parker is a 1989 Bay 16.2 hand stallion sired by Rugged Lark. Regal Lark is a 3-Time World Champion, a 4-Time Congress Champion and a Reserve Superhorse.*

*(middle photo)*
*Joyful Lark, now owned by Sidney Laney, the daughter of Buddy Laney, was Carol's favorite Heading and Heeling mare. Ridden by Robbie Schroeder, she is pictured winning at the 1990 Congress with Joan Schroeder and Jay Wadhams.*

*(bottom photo)*
*Mike & Marilyn Corrington, Carol Harris and Lynn Palm celebrate Rugged Lark's second Superhorse title.*

Green Working Hunter and World Champion Junior Working Hunter to win the illustrious Superhorse title at the World Show. Then, the next year, The Lark Ascending returned to become the 1992 World Champion Senior Working Hunter.

Nineteen ninety-four brought Rugged Lark the start of his television career as a featured star on the national show, 'In the Company of Animals'.

The following year Rugged Lark was given the supreme honor of being named the American Quarter Horse Association's Ambassador to the United States Equestrian Team and asked to perform at the Olympic Trials being held in Gladstone, New Jersey.

Carol could hardly believe the incredible ride this horse was giving her. The plain little bay colt that she couldn't sell was taking her on flights of fancy that she could never have imagined...from futurities to Superhorse; from Reddick, Florida, to national television; from conformation model to historic sire, and now to the Olympic Trials as proud representative of the entire American Quarter Horse Association. Owning Rugged Lark was like living a fairytale!

Little did she know what more the legend held in store....

*(top photo)*
*The Lark Ascending receives his 1991 Super Horse Award. Owned by Janet Reid and Ethel Strach.*

*(bottom photo)*
*The Lark Ascending and Michelle Grubb winning on the AHSA Circuit in Working Hunter in 1993 at Lake Placid.*

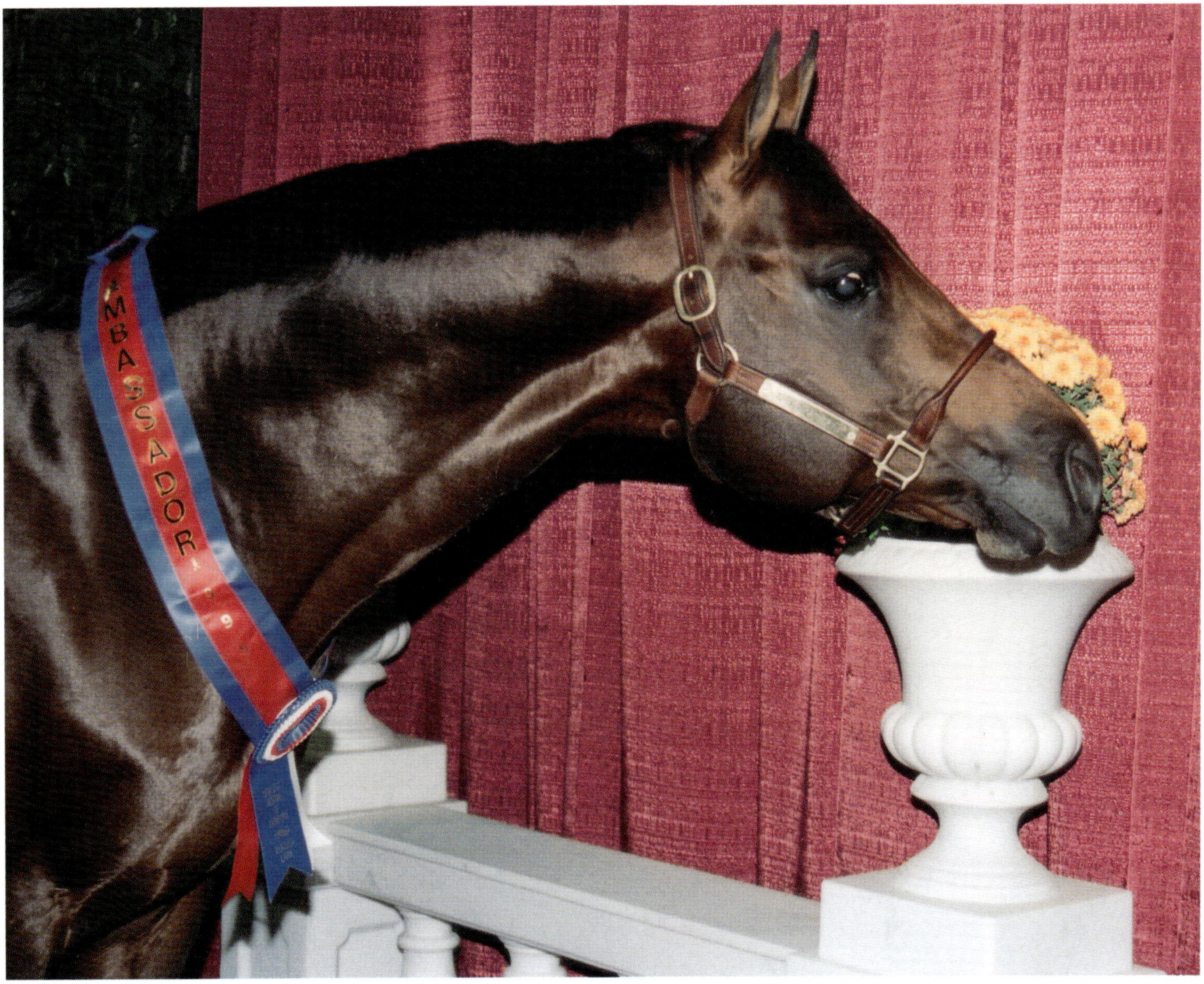


©courtesy of The Quarter Horse Journal

©Frank Flynn

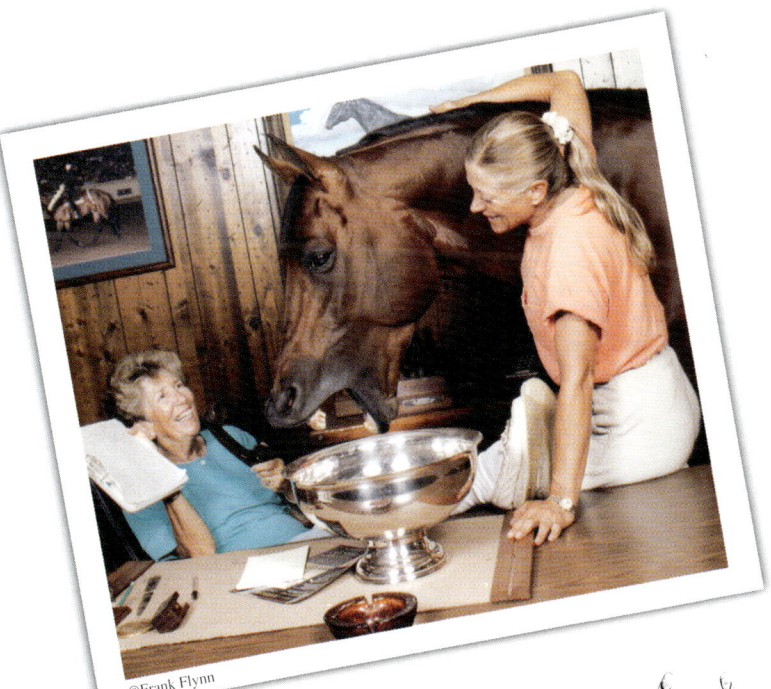

*(top photo)*
*Rugged Lark wears his ambassador's ribbon with pride at the 1995 All American Quarter Horse Congress where he signed autographs to benefit the U.S. Equestrian Team.*

*(bottom photo)*
*Lark is wowed by his invitation to become the ambassador to the USET.*

Dear Mrs. Harris,
  I love your horse, Rugged Lark. I did a report on him in school. It was very good. Please send me more information on him.
  I am in the 6th grade at Swanville School.

    Jessica R. Frieler

Dear Mr. Lark,
  I'm sure you would like to be friends with me. I am 15.3 hands and I'm an Arab-Quarter cross. I do training-level dressage. I hope to see you next year at the shows.

    Love,
    Lord Grey

Dear Two-Time Superhorse Rugged Lark,
  I could spot you in the dark. As silly as it may seem, I love to dream. To dream of a farm or park, especially to dream of Rugged Lark, so beautiful, yet so smart, with so much heart, I loved you from the start, and intend to love you to the end.

    Madelyn Fanini
    Doylestown, PA

To Carol Parker-Harris,
  Thank you for showing us your wonderful farm and especially your horses! When I first arrived, I saw Rugged Lark playing in the field and I felt like I was seeing a movie star behind the scenes.

    Sincerely,
    Holly Saigo,
    Independence, La.

Carol,
  Guess what? I was in D.C. last week with my mother and saw some of Lark's Breyer toys in the Smithsonian. I was impressed! What a star!

    Sue Page

Dear Rugged Lark,
  You're my favorite Quarter Horse stallion. I really, really missed you at the Congress this year. Last year I had my picture taken with you. When I am eleven, Mom is going to get me a Rugged Lark baby.
  When I get him, I will take care of him and love him. I'm 8 now.

    Love,
    Tara Taggart
    PA

Dear Carol & Rugged Lark,
  I am Rugged Lark's largest and most devoted fan in Tennessee. My name is Andrew Stooksberry and I am 15 years old. I want to know if you are going to appear in the southern part of Tennessee near Waynesboro. I hope so. My special thanks to Rugged Lark, he is a superhorse times two.

    Sincerely,
    Andrew Stooksberry

Dear Carol,
Thank you for the picture of Rugged Lark. Yes it fits on my wall. I put it right by my bed.

    Love,
    Zora Gwaniger - PA

Dear Mrs. Harris,
   All my children were deeply impressed by your knowledge and enthusiasm. They need role models to inspire them.

Gratefully,
Susan H. Drag
7th Grade Teacher
North Marion Middle School

Dear Mrs. Harris,
Thank you for letting me sit on Rugged Lark.
Your friend,
Rocky Santa Crus
Brandon, Fl.

Dear Carol,
   How is Lark? I am sending you a picture.
(Drawing of Lark in tall grass)

Your friend,
Savannah

Dear Mrs. Harris,
I'm writing to tell you what a wonderful horse you have. I had to do a research program and give a speech in front of my English class. I did my speech about your horse, Rugged Lark.
Jamie D. Widrig

Back in 1960, when Carol hauled my horse, Hollywood Snapper, and me to the Fort Worth Fat Stock Show to compete in the open cutting, Windy Ryon replied that if anyone from Ohio won the Fort Worth Cutting, he would give them a pair of silver engraved spurs. The spurs arrived in the mail a few weeks later. I've never forgotten this. Thanks, Carol.

Dale Wilkinson, Trainer

Dear Carol,
   We will never forget your exhibition at USET headquarters. It made us so proud to be Quarter Horse lovers.

June and Connie Ferrate

"Ho! Hum! Craig puts me to sleep every time he uses the rasp."

Wendy keeps the records straight and always with a smile.

"You are a very special person and we have been blessed for the time we have been able to spend with you. Wendy, you are so dear and a wonderful daughter. It would be very hard for your mother if she didn't have you to rely on at the farm when she has to be away."

Nancy Folck,
Breeder and National Equine Sales

Entrance photo by ©Reg Corkum

*Carol's sense of humor, integrity and dedication to the American Quarter Horse has made an impact to be remembered. A gracious lady and a great stallion.*

*Ken Smith*
*AQHA Past President*

**Wendy makes sure Lark stays fit.**     **Carol tries him with no bridle.**

*"Hey Dad - Is That You Down There?"*

*Mike Corrington remembered Lark when he was young, "He'd stand off by himself and just watch. He had a real unusual way of holding his head - down and kinda cocked."*

# THREE VERY SPECIAL GIRLS.

*Wendy, Allison, and Robin*

*All riding two-year-olds.*

*Some might say it was luck that Carol raised a horse like Lark, not so. She dreamed of and bred for that type of horse every time she made a breeding decision. Carol's true love of our Quarter Horse, and the people in it, is unequaled. She makes me laugh and she taught me so much.*

*Robin Merrill, Windward Stud*

They say that animals take on the personality of the people around them. If this is true, there is no doubt that Rugged Lark was destined to be a Champion. To see Carol and Rugged Lark together is seeing a very special friendship.

Jim & Bonnie Persinger

©Mary Phelps

# Chapter Eight
# One Moment In Time
## *"From Superhorse to Superstar"*

Returning from judging the annual Michigan Quarter Horse Futurity, Carol trudged wearily down the concourse of Atlanta's International Airport to check the monitor for the departure gate of her connection to Gainesville. While in Michigan, she'd purchased an Italian Greyhound puppy she'd needed to fortify her breeding program and was anxious to get the little guy settled in at home. Locating her flight number, she was dismayed by the annoying notice flashing beside it: "Delayed".

"Shoot! Hours to kill...may as well get comfortable while we wait," she sighed, turning back to the sky-lounge she'd just passed. Placing the tiny dog crate gently on the counter, she climbed onto the cushy leather stool and ordered a snack and drink. Looming over the bar, the television offered non-stop coverage of the 1988 Olympics taking place in Seoul, Korea.

The puppy was getting restless, so she opened the crate to stroke it reassuringly. Suddenly, her attention was drawn to the TV screen as Whitney Houston sang the new Olympic theme, 'One Moment in Time'. As the lyrics flowed, Carol was stunned by the incredibly personal message they delivered.

*Each day I live*
*I want to be*
*A day to give the best of me*
*I'm only one*
*But not alone, my finest days are yet unknown*
*...I rise and fall*
*Yet through it all*
*This much remains*
*I want one moment in time*
*When I'm more than I thought I could be*
*When all of my dreams are a heartbeat away*
*And the answers are all up to me*
*Give me one moment in time*
*When I'm racing with destiny*
*Then in that one moment in time*
*I will feel, I will feel eternity*
*I've lived to be the very best*
*I want it all, no time for less*
*I've laid my plans*
*Now lay the chance here in my hands*
*You're a winner for a lifetime*
*If you seize that one moment in time*
*Make it shine*
*Give me one moment in time*
*When I'm racing with destiny*
*Then, in that one moment in time*
*I will be...free!*

© 1988 Albert Hammond Music (ASCAP), John Bettis Music (ASCAP), WB Music Corp. (ASCAP)

It was as if the song had been written about Rugged Lark!

Due to the excitement Lark's surprise Superhorse Award had generated at the 1987 World Show, the AQHA had recently called Carol to ask if she'd be willing to have Rugged Lark do an exhibition for the 1988 Congress in October.

And now here, in a bar in the bustling Atlanta Airport, Carol finds the perfect words and music presented to her, because she was forced to stop and wait for a delayed flight. Once again, inspiration materialized from the mysterious either as fate? ...kismet? ...coincidence? and caused Carol to detour in time to hear the music that would become Rugged Lark's signature song.

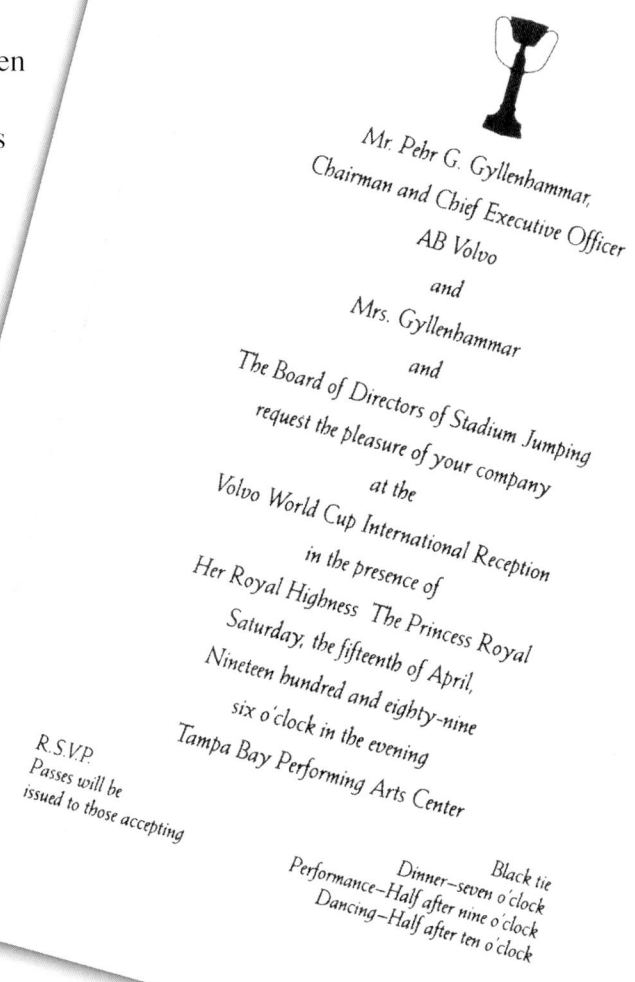

Carol and Lynn choreographed a Western Reining routine for the 1988 All American Quarter Horse Congress in which Lynn begins working with Lark to John Williams' flourishing fanfare, 'Olympic Spirit'. When that piece ends, Lynn dismounts, removes his bridle, delivers it to Carol and returns to finish the ride, bridleless, to the Whitney Houston song.

Both women were pleased with the stirring routine but were totally unprepared for the reaction it produced. The audience found the exhibition so moving that by the end there was hardly a dry eye in the house.

Amazed by the profoundly emotional reaction Rugged Lark's performance stirred up, Carol figured it was probably due to being at the Congress with its' audience made up of many life-long friends, competitors, and business associates. This "hometown crowd" had watched Lark go from a young Reining favorite to two-time Superhorse and were now inspired by the stallion's expanding success. Whatever the reason behind it, the reaction was real, remarkable, and rewarding, for Carol realized that through Rugged Lark people were appreciating equine spirit in a new, uniquely personal way. Lark's performance represents the best of both equine freedom and interspecies cooperation. This combination touches something deep in the human heart—the connection with another species is so fragile, yet so vital, that when we witness such mutual respect and unbridled trust, our heart literally sings and tears of joy flood our soul.

Nineteen eighty-nine was also the year Rugged Lark was invited to perform at the Volvo World Cup competition when it came to Tampa, Florida. An exciting international event, it was being held in Tampa's enormous football stadium. Carol and Lynn were a bit anxious about Rugged Lark's reaction to the sheer

size of that arena, the noise of fourteen bands that were scattered around the stadium, plus the distracting motion and general cacophony of thousands of spectators. This was by far the largest, loudest and most chaotic venue they'd ever taken on.

When the time for their performance arrived, Lynn had resigned herself to fate deciding that if she ever trusted Lark to do as he should, this was the time she needed to muster that trust once again.

The first half of the show went well, but as she dismounted after the completion of the Olympic Spirit routine to take his bridle off, she realized how incredibly far away Carol was standing, waiting to receive it. As usual, she had halted Rugged Lark at the center of the arena, but this "arena" was huge, so the centerpoint was the fifty-yard line and Carol seemed to be miles away. Lynn would have to leave Lark standing for a looonnng time while she walked the bridle over to Carol. Praying that he'd still be there upon her return, she didn't dare look up until she was all the way back. Miraculously, except for a couple of yawns and a relaxing shimmy-shake, Lark had stood still...as Carol notes, "...like an obedience dog on a long stay."

With a tremendous sigh of relief, Lynn remounted and completed the bridleless routine with flair and renewed pride in her exceptional partner. Little did she realize that the true test of Lark's equilibrium was yet to come.

*(top left) Rugged Lark performing at the Volvo World Cup in Tampa, Florida. An exciting international event, it was held in Tampa's enormous football stadium.*

*(bottom right) He stood there "like an obedience dog on a long stay."*

Among the renowned horse enthusiasts attending was Britain's Princess Anne who had unfortunately arrived late and missed Rugged Lark's exhibition. Hearing how extraordinary it was, and being of royal blood, she thought little of requesting that they do it again. Lark and Lynn generously complied, thrilling the Princess with a most memorable command performance after the competitions were completed.

As the final presenter on the program, Lynn and Lark remained front and center while the Grand Finale of the 1989 Volvo World Cup was announced. Lynn couldn't believe what was happening, yet had little choice but to stand rooted to the center of the arena as every single horse and rider that participated in the event joined them. Soon there were literally hundreds of hunters, jumpers, mounted patrols, carriage horses, Arabians, Appaloosas, Morgans, Paints, Paso Fino's, and all the Grand Prix horses surrounding them. Lynn and Lark found themselves in the middle of a literal sea of nervous, dancing horseflesh. Then the coup de grace: on cue, all fourteen bands struck up an earth-shaking rendition of "God Bless America!"

Like a cannon shot, that triggered equine bedlam as the high-strung, athletic Grand Prix horses bumped into one another, while other mounts pranced and pitched and begged to go home...now!

In all that swirling-dervish action, attention was drawn to the calm in the center of the storm. Steady as a clock, Rugged Lark stood surveying the chaos—the only horse not moving and the only mount without a bridle! The crowd was impressed, Lynn was relieved, and Carol was proud as a mother hen.

Bob Standish, Executive Director of the United States Equestrian Team (USET) knew of Rugged Lark's exhibitions and asked to have him perform at the 1989 Festival of Champions. This Festival is held each June at USET headquarters in Gladstone, New Jersey, to showcase the top dressage, jumping, eventing, and driving competitors. Carol and Lynn decided to revamp the performance for this elite audience. Switching from Western to English tack, Lynn set aside her dazzling western costume for a formal dressage habit with just a touch of sassy sequins. They raised the bar on the act as well, adding more advanced haute école dressage moves, plus jumping, to the bridleless routine.

Gladstone represents the pinnacle of English equestrian sports in the United States. Formerly a private estate, the expansive grounds are meticulously maintained with formal, manicured gardens surrounding the imposing brick Georgian mansion. As their rig negotiated the long driveway toward the impressive stucco and brick stables, Carol hugged the Whippet on her lap and quipped, "Well, Toto, we're sure not in Kansas anymore...."

As soon as they unloaded Lark, Carol began laughing, "Wow, it's like he was shrunk at the cleaners!" Here was her beautifully-turned-out Quarter Horse stallion suddenly surrounded by the huge warmbloods and tall, muscled Thoroughbreds so prevalent in English events. Lark's 15:2 1/2-hand stature suddenly seemed paltry next to these seventeen- and eighteen-hand giants.

"Now don't you worry, Lark," she whispered reassuringly, "We obviously can't score in the height department, so we'll just have to show them what a Quarter Horse can do."

Her tone was confident although her mind was beginning to raise doubts...would this crowd even be interested in what they had to offer? There wasn't another Quarter Horse in sight, and Carol knew that breed prejudice is a strong, and at times, a derisively dividing element in equestrian sport. Away from the comfortable, familiar Quarter Horse show environment,

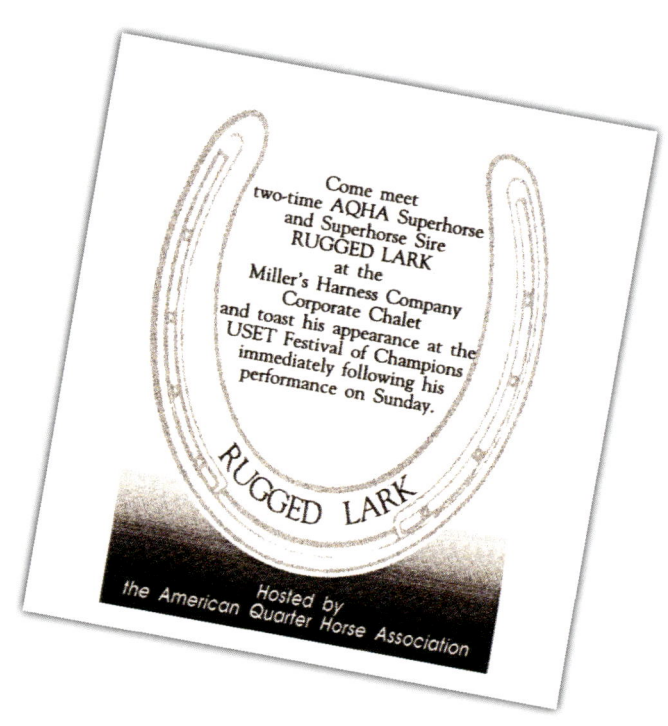

©Bob Tarr

©courtesy of AQHA

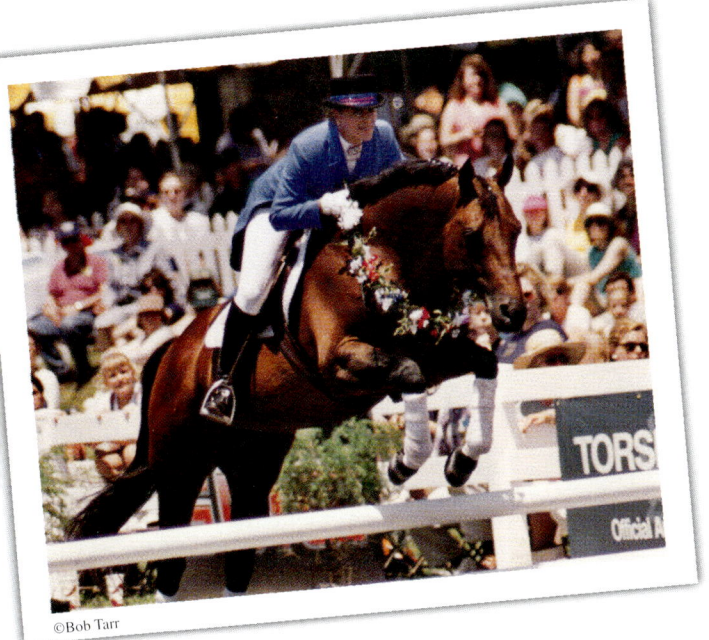

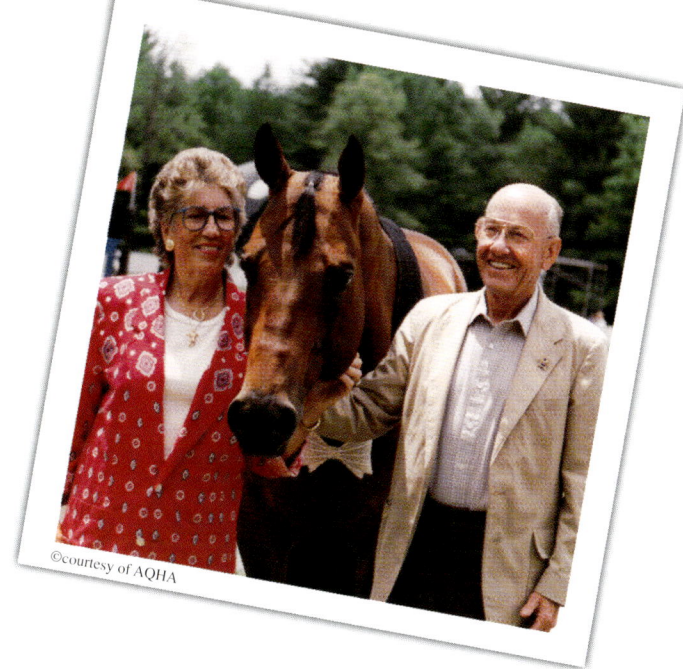

*(top right photo)*
*Delvin Miller, a hall of fame harness horseman, came to see Rugged Lark and Carol at the 1989 Festival of Champions*
*(top left and bottom photos)*
*Rugged Lark performing at the 1989 Festival of Champions.*
*This festival is held each June at USET headquarters in Gladstone, New Jersey.*

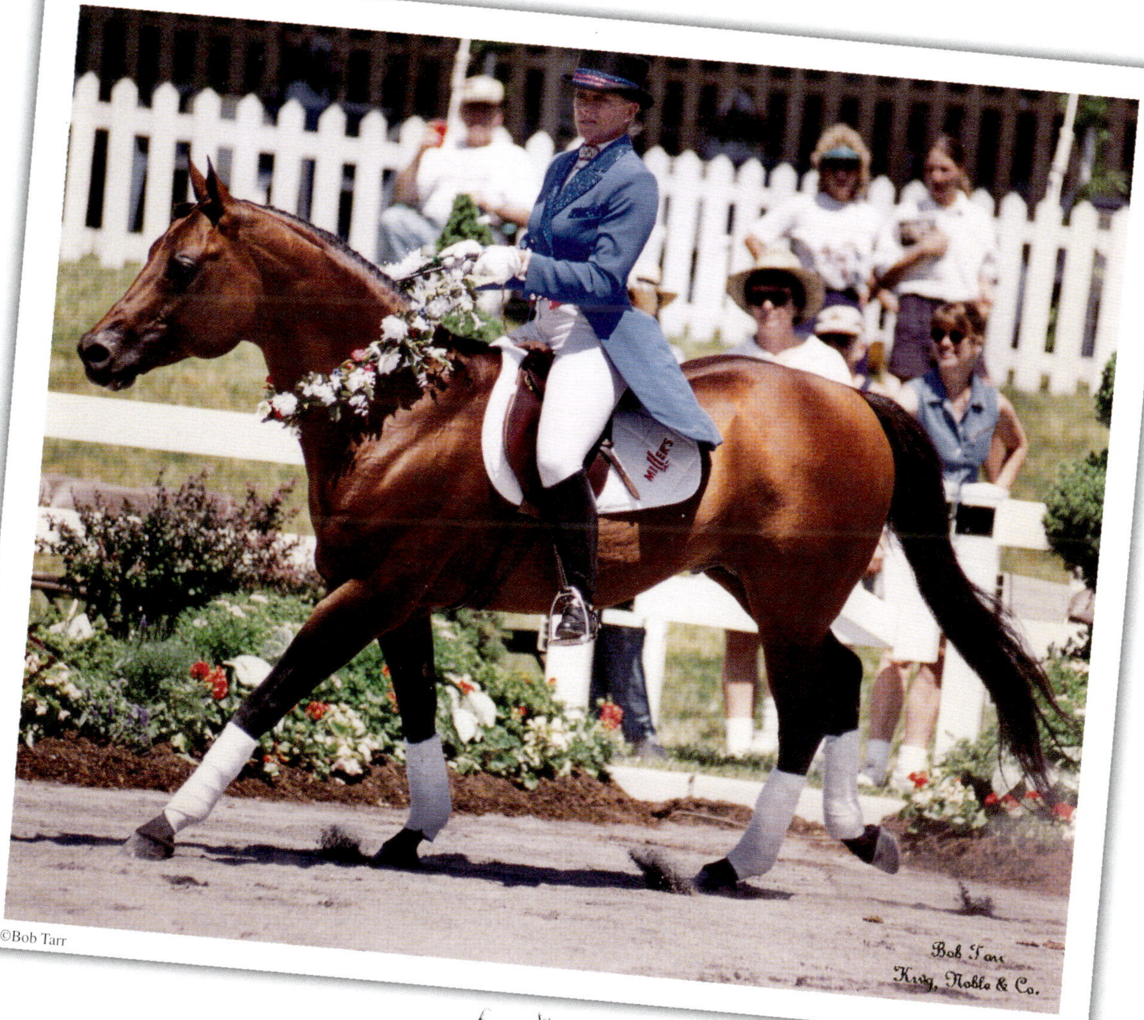


©Bob Tarr

*This Rugged Lark exhibition finale left him sitting with Lynn, Carol and Allison. He left the crowd on it's feet.*

Carol suddenly felt adrift and a bit alone, not at all sure of what reception to expect. "Well, we'll just do our best and hope for the best," she thought.

Her anxiety was quelled when the first of Rugged Lark's two Gladstone performances was announced and the dressage arena bleachers filled rapidly...obviously they were interested! Before the last note was played, this select crowd of talented equestrians was on their feet cheering, clambering for more...and yes, once again, many were crying with the sheer joy of it all! It was now clear that all who witnessed Rugged Lark's performance were caught in its magical spell.

Hunter-jumper trainer Colleen McQuay recalls her reaction, "I'm a professional with a long career in which I've done a lot with horses, but that initial performance at Gladstone was the first time I saw Rugged Lark do his complete routine. My daughter was also at Gladstone then and won the Talent Derby; but I cried more watching Rugged Lark than when my daughter won! I'll always remember that 'moment in time'."

"I think Lark's performance touches people for different reasons," Colleen continues. "As a horse trainer, I have personal ties to him, but I think the most amazing thing is just seeing what a horse gives willingly to man."

*(top right)*
*Carol and Lark with friend,*
*Jackie Gaudio, at the Feed Store Party.*

*(top Left)*
*Marilyn Crabb, Bill Ellis and Wendell Armstrong*
*at the Feed Store Party.*

USET Director, Bob Standish, was asked why he thought Rugged Lark's performance elicited such emotion when it's not much different from a Kur—a dressage routine set to music—which are performed regularly in competition. "Everyone just becomes so emotionally involved with this horse," Bob observed. "I see a lot of people crying, and I think it's in absolute appreciation of the fact that this horse can do so much and relates so well to his trainers. When Rugged Lark performs, it's always a very sentimental occasion."

Since the word was out that this was a not-to-be-missed-experience, Lark's remaining show was scheduled for the larger Grand Prix arena. As Sue Page reports, "The big arena held all the huge, colorful jumps including one with Shamu The Killer Whale on both sides of it. When the first musical routine ended, Lynn dismounted as usual, took off Lark's bridle, walked over to Carol, handed her the bridle and walked back to Lark. But this time, Rugged Lark, The Superhorse, added a new twist to the act...he ducked out."

Having passed the test with flying colors at the World Cup exhibition, for some reason Lark felt the need to take off at Gladstone. Carol laughs at the memory, "Lark simply 'left town'. He cantered over to the in-gate where his groom, George Miles was standing. George led him back to us and whispered, 'He thinks you're gonna make him jump that Shamu thing.'"

Though George's theory fits as well as any, Lark's change of heart was just another reminder that even with his remarkable consistency, we have a ways to go before mastering the equine psyche.

"Carol was kind of embarrassed," Sue remembers, "but a very professional man reminded us, 'Look, we have to remember he is a horse, and he is a stallion and things happen.'"

Rugged 95 Lark

Rugged 96 Lark

*(opposite page)*
*Rugged Lark looking elegant in his custom designed black-tie and french cuffs.*

*(top left)*
*Don Treadway, Ambassador Lark, and guests at the AQHA Olympic Party.*

*(top right)*
*Carol's grandchildren, Wendell and Summer, meet U.S. Olympic stars David and Karen O'Connor.*

"And that's so true," Sue concurs. "Lark is not an automated character. He is a horse...an awesome horse."

Despite Lark's digression, the applause was tremendous. For this savvy crowd understood that Lark's wayward behavior only underscored how remarkable his normally consistent control is, since he obviously obeys in spite of a desire to kick up his heels or show fear like any healthy horse.

The crowd's endorsement and ensuing bond of respect, friendship and mutual love of the horse following Lark's performances at Gladstone so delighted Lynn and Carol that they wanted to show how very appreciative they were. True to her spontaneous nature, Carol decided to demonstrate their appreciation by bringing a surprise celebrity escort to the gala black-tie reception at the Gladstone mansion that evening.

Arriving socially late, heads turned and excited waves of conversation swept over the gathering as Carol and her famous escort climbed the flagstone steps leading to the lighted garden terrace. Carol was glorious in a long, teal-blue chiffon gown that fluttered gently around her in the evening breeze. Her tall, dark and handsome escort, looking elegant in his custom designed black-tie and french cuffs, walked confidently beside her.

No need for introductions here...the name of this super athlete was as well-known to the crowd as Joe Montana, Magic Johnson, Nolan Ryan or Arnold Palmer. Rugged Lark, once again bridleless, but now wearing formal attire, was the hit of Gladstone's Festival of Champions' gala affaire.

Carol, Lynn and Lark returned to the USET's Festival of Champions at Gladstone in 1995 to perform proudly under the auspicious title of Goodwill Ambassador for the American Quarter Horse Association. This time, however, Carol walked out to center ring between the two routines and removed Lark's bridle while Lynn remained in the saddle, for Shamu The Whale was still watching.

The next year, the AQHA named Rugged Lark their Official Ambassador to the 1996 Olympics in Atlanta, so Carol, Lynn and Lark gave a final triumphant performance at Gladstone during the USET Olympic Trials.

Then it was on to the Olympics in Georgia!

Long-time friends of Carol's, Marilyn and David Crabb, graciously opened their home to Rugged Lark's entourage. Since they lived right in Conyers, Georgia, where the Olympic equestrian events were taking place, it was a tremendous logistical advantage. The Crabbs arranged for Rugged Lark to be stabled nearby and then they hosted a packed reception for Lark's friends and fans at their local feed store.

"The Olympics were really fun because, unlike other shows, it was such a family affair," notes Lynn Palm. "Carol's daughter, Allison, came with her children, Summer and Wendell; my husband, Cyril Pittion-Rossillon, myself and another professional in the hunter-jumper world, Bill Ellis, came with us, and we just had a grand time. It was like a vacation...one horse and all the family."

Being the largest registry and most popular breed in the world, the American Quarter Horse was well represented by a number of talented individuals including Rex Peterson and his liberty horse, and Doc's Keepin' Time, star of the 1994 remake of Black Beauty, as well as many other movies and television shows.

"Over the two weeks of the Olympics, they had other Quarter Horses demonstrating the versatility of the breed with Cutting, Barrel-racing, and Charro exhibitions," Lynn recalls, "but as the official Ambassador of the AQHA, Rugged Lark represented the all-around American home-bred kind of horse. So there was real pride in that we were out there representing and promoting the American Quarter Horse with a very special one...that was the Olympic highlight for me."

"The height of the seating area was visible from a good distance," notes Lynn, "so you just knew there were a lot of people. Since Rugged Lark and I were doing solo performances, all those eyes were going to be watching us, and I had to really prepare myself

*(top photo) Two AQHA Silver Spur award winners, Rugged Lark and Doc's Keepin Time, better known as Black Beauty, meet once again at the Olympics.*
*(middle and bottom photos) Rugged Lark performing at the 1996 Summer Olympics.*

mentally so as not to get too nervous. But since I'd already had so much excitement and experience with this horse, that was pretty easy."

The weather did not cooperate the day of their second Olympic performance. The flags snapped and strained in the wind as the sky darkened ominously. By the time they stepped into the arena, showers had begun, but Lynn looked past the beautifully planted display of the Olympic's woven-ring symbol to a surprisingly full house...no rain-checks wanted here. Umbrellas popped open like mushrooms in compost, but the spectators sat glued to their damp seats for the entire performance. The final notes brought another standing ovation for Lynn and Lark—this time whipped by a frenzy of national pride as Americans and foreigners alike waved flags and roared approval in the rain.

This time, Lynn was the one who cried with joy....

In November of 1996, acknowledging Rugged Lark's valuable goodwill and undeniable showmanship, the AQHA bestowed the Silver Spur Award "In recognition of his contributions as an ambassador and entertainer." Although the Silver Spur has recently been made an annual award, at the time Lark was honored, it was only presented as merited, with Lark being just the fourth in AQHA history to receive it.

With such an unprecedented string of national and international honors and his exploding popularity, it was now apparent that Rugged Lark's fame had rocketed beyond the realm of AQHA Superhorse to International Superstar!

Realizing how rarely such a special horse with so many incredible accomplishments comes along, Bayer Animal Health arranged with the AQHA to sponsor a retirement tour of five major equestrian venues, bringing "The Magic of Rugged Lark" to

*(top photo) The AQHA bestowed the Silver Spur Buckle and Award on Lark "In recognition of his contributions as an ambassador and entertainer."*
*(middle photo) Rugged Lark witnesses the signing of his contract with Marve Jahde for the Bayer Corporation's sponsorship of his Farewell Tour.*
*(bottom photo) Carol Harris is inducted into the AQHA Hall of Fame in 1997.*

Rugged 99 Lark

*Carol, with daughter Allison, at the Hall Of Fame induction in Dallas, Texas.*

tens of thousands of horse lovers in 1997.

In March of that same year, Carol Harris was honored for her career achievements by being inducted into the American Quarter Horse Association's Hall of Fame. At the induction banquet during her acceptance speech, Carol shared some of her professional beliefs with that enthusiastic gathering:

Her belief that the "Quarter Horse is the best breed of horse in the world."

Her belief "in work with no shortcuts," especially when working with animals that depend on us 365 days a year.

Her belief in "fun and keeping things light...to avoid pressures because pressures invite mistakes and mistakes invite failure."

Her belief in respecting rules to help us stay on course.

Her belief in equestrian education—"not just for our kids, but for judges, trainers, spectators...and the public at large."

*Rugged Lark made an unforgettable appearance at the 1997 Florida Reining Horse Classic in Ocala, Florida. The show created a full-blown traffic jam.*

Her belief that there is room for improvement in the training and judging of rail horses.

Her belief in responsible breeding to prevent over-breeding or in-breeding of popular bloodlines.

Her belief that the AQHA has the talent and effective leadership to continue on its inspired path now and on into the future.

And finally her profound belief that she was, at that moment, "the happiest and proudest lady alive."

She also had to have been a happy and proud lady when Rugged Lark and Lynn made their final appearance at the 1997 Florida Reining Horse Classic in neighboring Ocala, Florida. "That show created a full-blown traffic jam!" reports Keith Bradley. "I'm serious as a heartbeat—there were so many trying to get in that we had to hold up the show to let everybody in that could get in. They finally stopped selling tickets because making change was taking too long and they were out of seats anyway, so they just let folks pass. It was really a great event."

"Bill Horn, The National Reining Horse Association's leading money earner, was there," Keith recalls. "So after Lynn and Lark did their English routine, while Carol's out there waving to the crowd, I called to her over the mike, 'Carol, can he rein? Bill Horn's here and if we can find a saddle, let's see....'"

"So they put a western saddle on Lark, Bill took a couple of laps around the pen, loosened him up and asked him to give us a sliding stop...he slid about 25 feet! It was just absolute beauty—a pair of champions together. Oh boy, what a thrill!"

"Bill had ridden him a little bit that afternoon to kinda get acquainted," explains Keith, "but it didn't take a whole lot of acquaintance. It's amazing to me how great riders can get on a horse and the acquaintance is so quick and so short...they're working together like a team so fast it just absolutely blows my mind. A good horseman knows when he's straddled a good horse; they know what to expect, they know how to react, and how to work together. It's fantastic!"

Bo-Bett's farrier, Craig Renwick was at that event and was struck by the transformation he witnessed in Rugged Lark between the two performances, "When Lynn was on him, he was in one mode, so when Bill Horn got on him, I thought, 'This could be a mistake—he'll just plug around like a dressage horse.'

*Rugged Lark at Devon Horse Show in Devon, Pennsylvania.*

But all at once he became excitable...he really woke up. Bill galloped him around a bit, then asked him to slide and he did a beautiful slide. He was really on fire!"

"I'd never seen a change like that in a horse before—in a split second...you could see that he knows who's got the hands on him and performs to their satisfaction. It was really something to watch. It was very dynamic and got everybody really excited!"

Shortly after that hometown appearance, it was time to hit the road with Rugged Lark's Farewell Tour sponsored by Bayer Animal Health.

The first stop was the historic Devon Horse Show in Devon, Pennsylvania, where Rugged Lark wound up being stabled among the exotically beautiful Friesian horses. Even constant rains couldn't dampen the wonderfully warm reception Lark received as headlines in the Philadelphia Inquirer proclaimed, "Retiree Steals Show In Devon" - Super Quarter Horse Rugged Lark wowed them on his last tour.

That banner headline was such a publicity coup for the American Quarter Horse, that to this day Leslie Baker has it framed in her office.

The next stop brought Rugged Lark back to Louisville, Kentucky, site of his Reining Pre-Futurity win fourteen years before. This time he was featured at "The Mane Event", the exciting entertainment extravaganza of the Equitana USA exhibition. As Leslie Baker, AQHA coordinator of the Bayer Tour recalls, "At Equitana's Mane Event, in Louisville's Exposition Hall, Rugged Lark was so 'on' that the crowd gave him several standing ovations."

The August venue was the famous Hampton Classic, near the tip of New York's Long Island. This show attracts the rich and famous from all over the country...and beyond. Carol was relieved that a friend on Long Island offered the use of a travel trailer, and honored that, as the owner of

Phila. Inquirer 5/28/97

**Young admirers flock around** Rugged Lark during his last show in Devon. The horse has twice won the American Quarter Horse Association World Championship Superhorse title. His owner says he's too valuable to take on the road any longer.

For The Inquirer / JOAN FAIR

# Retiree steals show in Devon

Courtesy of The Philadelphia Inquirer

*(top photo)*
*Rugged Lark makes the headlines in The Philadelphia Inquirer where it proclaimed, "Retiree Steals Show In Devon" - Super Quarter Horse Rugged Lark wowed them on his last tour.*

*(left)*
*Carol with John Rotz, the Hall of Fame Jockey who rode Lark's dad, Really Rugged, at Belmont Park.*

AQHA invites you to toast Rugged Lark on his 1997 Farewell Tour during The Mane Event.

DATE: Friday, June 20, 1997
LOCATION: Ste. V-1 at Freedom Hall

Rugged 103 Lark

(top photo)
*Rugged Lark goes back to Louisville, Kentucky, site of his Reining Pre-Futurity win fourteen years before. This time he was featured at "The Mane Event", the exciting entertainment extravaganza of the Equitana USA exhibition.*
(top left and left photos)
*Rugged Lark makes new friends with "Looney Tunes," the Llama and "Sweetie Pie," the Miniature Horse filly.*

one of the star attractions, she'd be allowed to stay on the show grounds, gratis. The rest of Lark's entourage was just a touch envious of this royal arrangement since they were all having to scramble to find rooms scattered around the island.

Usually Carol hauls her own horses to shows, but since getting to Long Island required threading a complicated trail through New York City, she hired an experienced truck driver who knew the best and safest routes. So she and Lark arrived with their "chauffeur", rested and ready to enjoy the rarified atmosphere of the Hampton Classic.

After getting Rugged Lark settled into his stall, Carol and Marv Jahde, Bayer's Equine Products Manager, went in search of her home away from home. Marv couldn't help laughing when they found it, "It was parked down where they stored tractor-trailers, and dumped the trash and used shavings from the stables...."

Marv recalls with a chuckle, "We teased Carol a lot about living in the 'hood' at the Hamptons!"

As it turned out, Carol looked on the bright side and had the last laugh, "I admit the scenery was not great, but the convenience was first class. The trailer was comfortable, I was close to Lark, and the price was right!"

Dreams of grandeur aside, all had a full and fun few days presenting to appreciative audiences, playing hookey at the beach, and enjoying the neighboring Llamas and an adorable Miniature filly with whom Rugged Lark fell in love. Being a Miniature horse driving and racing enthusiast, Carol even looked into the possibility of purchasing Lark's newest girlfriend, but had to decline due to her healthy *(right photos) Carol's home away from home in the Hamptons. A friend on Long Island offered Carol the use of a travel trailer for the event. Carol was teased a lot about living in the 'hood' in the Hamptons!"*

price of $30,000! Seems Lark's as good a judge of quality as Carol.

October brought Rugged Lark's Farewell Tour to the familiar surroundings of the All American Quarter Horse Congress. After another rousing performance, crowds of fans swarmed around Lark, Lynn, and Carol. Eddie Cridge, a Reining trainer and AQHA judge Carol has known for many years was waiting at the out-gate with his young daughter.

"Eddie is a great guy who I didn't think had a serious bone in his body," Carol reports. "He's just always kidding. But when he came up to me after Lark's performance, he was a different man. He said, 'Carol, that brought out something in me I didn't even know was there.... There ain't a horse in the world that could make me cry, but all of a sudden, there I was, just sobbing, watching that horse!'"

"Then he asked, 'Would it be all right for my little girl to sit on him?'"

"I said, 'Certainly,'...and he took pictures and I took pictures.... I was really touched by Eddie."

For many it seems watching Rugged Lark perform is akin to finding a geode. At first glance it doesn't seem so very different from many other rocks... But suddenly, it breaks open, revealing a totally unexpected, scintillating inner beauty that touches us deeply. It's utterly amazing that so ordinary a form contains such a wealth of glittering treasure. Thus, Rugged Lark's performance makes us marvel, and wondrously grateful for the privilege of witnessing the seamless melding of two disparate spirits into one delightful, dancing centaur. Lark's joyously unfettered presence is magical, it's mythical, and it makes grown men cry.

*Don Treadway and Carol wait for a table at an elegant restaurant in the Hamptons.*

*Carol enjoying a quick trip to the beach while in the Hamptons.*

*The August venue was the famous Hampton Classic, near the tip of New York's Long Island. This show attracts the rich and famous from all over the country...and beyond. They loved Rugged Lark.*

*Supermodel Christie Brinkley came to see Rugged Lark at the Hampton Classic, and signed his picture. He thought she was more than beautiful.*

### American Quarter Horse
# Rugged Lark
with owner Carol Harris
and trainer Lynn Palm Pittion-Rossillon

*To Rugged Lark — love + kisses from Christie Brinkley*

©Bayer Animal Health

# Chapter Nine
# Horse Play
### "Who's In The Horse Suit?"

One of the persistent impressions of Rugged Lark that crops up time and again is the comment that "someone's in there". Rugged Lark's reactions and responses are so often so very human that it seems there must be a person inside working the controls of a very well-constructed horse suit. With all the advances in special effects, computer imaging, and virtual realities nowadays, this possibility is not as far-fetched as one might think.

One who subscribes to this notion is artist Debbie Fitzgerald. Numerous photo sessions with Lark have led her to the conclusion that there's more here than mere horse sense: "It's never a dull moment taking pictures at Bo-Bett...trying to get pictures of eight puppies all in a row, which is simply unbelievable, or photographing Lark. That is always fun because he's got this sense, a special kind of intelligence about him...he's always alert and quite the ham."

"He's so smart about it—he thinks he's almost a person—and Carol treats him that way. For the first five or ten minutes he'll be very good, doing all these fabulous poses—exactly what you want...then he starts messing with you—he'll start yawning and will not stop. This goes beyond just a yawn—it's definitely messing with ya' because soon everyone around him is yawning and laughing. It's like he's saying, 'You're not going to get the picture you want, but here's some comic relief.' It's like he's laughing at you—and I think he is—I have a large collection of Lark laughing pictures."

"Another trick he pulls when he's bored with being photographed," says Debbie, "he starts dropping.... Carol is a riot with that! She gets him trotting, or takes a brush and bongs it a bit 'til Lark retracts it, but then he drops it right back down again—messing with us!"

"One time, when I was trying to get a photo

*(opposite page)*
*"ONE MOMENT IN TIME"*
*An oil painting of Rugged Lark*
*by Ocala artist Debbie Fitzgerald*
*"...he's got this sense, a special kind*
*of intelligence about him," she says.*

*(right photo)*
*Lynn and Lark receive roses at the National Horse Show.*

*(top photo)*
*Lark and Carol enjoy a moment answering the phone in the Bo-Bett office.*
*"Hey Butch it's for you!"*

*(bottom photo)*
*Rugged Lark's friend, Butch Campbell, says hello at the 1997 AQHA World Show.*

for the big oil painting I did, he simply would not pull it up. It wasn't breeding season—no mares around—but it's his way of saying, 'Been here, done this, I'm not in the mood....' So, we have this one classic picture of Carol actually holding it out of the way."

Butch Campbell, who helped trick-train Lark, relates another instance when a segment for the TV show, 'In the Company of Animals' was being shot at Bo-Bett. "This called for Lark to be lying down in the office awaiting a call. The phone was ringing on and off while Lark was laying there... Then, the one time they say they're going to shoot the take, the horse is laid out, the phone rings and Lark raises his head and looks at Carol as if to ask, 'Is that for me?'"

"He does things like that on most every promotional shoot he's done. It absolutely astounds people...like he knows exactly what Carol is saying or what he's supposed to do. He's absolutely the most human horse that I've ever been around."

While at Bo-Bett doing research for this book, the author had an experience that's made her join the camp of horse-suit believers. Rebekah asked for a picture with Rugged Lark, so Carol took her to the barn and called Lark...off his feed. He obligingly left his grain, came out of his stall, stopped while she gave him a quick brushing and oiled his hooves, then stood patiently next to Rebekah while Carol snapped away. At one point, Carol reminded Rebekah not to hold Lark's head, and as her hand came away, Carol cracked a joke that made her laugh. It wasn't until the film was developed that she discovered Lark was laughing at the joke as well! ...who is in there?

Carol loves to see her animals enjoying themselves, so she gives them many opportunities for play.

She has a wonderful home video of an energetic two-year-old son of Rugged Lark, Lieutenant Lark, playing with a ball in the round pen. This colt had enjoyed a horse ball in the pasture so much that Butch Campbell got a larger one for him...a huge four-footer! What a riot it is to watch this horse-colt go after that enormous orb. He attacks it with the exuberance of a British soccer star—hitting and pushing it with his head; he strikes at it, jumps on it, then rolls off it only to throw himself onto it once again! While most horses would freak at such a large, active, foreign object, Lieutenant Lark romps with it with courageous abandon and an athletic agility that is nothing short of amazing.

While the youngsters have fun in Bo-Bett's big, round playpen, their

*(top photo)*
*The author, Rebekah Witter, and Rugged Lark share a joke.*

*(bottom photo)*
*Some horses enjoy a ball and some could care less. A son of Rugged Lark who Carol named "Roy" loved this red ball.*

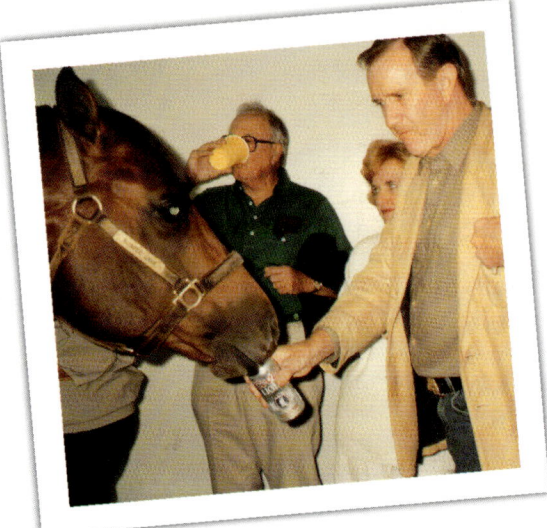

dad enjoys more sophisticated amusements, such as entertaining clients. As Nancy Folck explains, "After a sale we held at Bo-Bett in 1988, Carol ordered in a bunch of food to thank everyone. The next thing you know, she brings Lark in and turns him loose in the office—with no halter! He went around smelling everybody's plate like, 'What have you got to eat?' And when he found anybody who had champagne.... Boy! he had his tongue in your cup, slurping it up quicker than you could say, 'Hey, that's mine!'"

"We had some friends from Florida with us and they were absolutely amazed...they just couldn't believe he's just like a big dog! It's hard to describe, but Carol and Lark have a very special relationship."

Rugged Lark seems to have special relationships with a number of people, as his "drinking buddy", Bill Brewer, Executive Vice President of the AQHA relates, "For several years, a group of us have been trying

*(top right photo)* Stan Permowitz shares a beer with Rugged Lark at a party at Bo-Bett.

*(top left photo)* Lark checks his Superhorse Trophy for a treat. It usually is filled with champagne or Fiddle-Faddle®.

*(bottom photo)* An invitation to visit Rugged Lark at the 1989 Volvo World Cup.

---

You are cordially invited
to an
American Quarter Horse Association
reception honoring

**RUGGED LARK,**

the world's only two-time Superhorse
award winner

Wednesday, April 12, 1989
5 - 7 p.m.

AQHA International
Hospitality Village Chalet #28

to get Reining approved as an FEI sport and as an Olympic sport. Rugged Lark has been a big ambassador for us in trying to achieve this objective." [Their efforts were rewarded in April of 2000 when Reining was approved by the FEI as a competitive international sport.]

"In 1989, at the Volvo World Cup in Tampa, Florida, an FEI World competition for jumping horses," Bill continues, "we were trying to meet and greet people who were associated with traditional English riding, to get them accustomed to cowboy hats and the Western Reining event. Rugged Lark did his demonstration at the opening, so they saw him Rein and perform as a Quarter Horse."

"We had invited some VIP's to a reception that Don Treadway, Doris Barton and I helped host for the AQHA. Rugged Lark was there to greet the

*(top left photo) AQHA President Bill Englund presents Carol with a special trophy honoring Rugged Lark's participation in the 1989 Volvo World Cup.*

*(top right photo) Lynn Palm, Rugged Lark and Carol Harris on their way to the AQHA reception at the 1989 Volvo World Cup.*

*(bottom photo - left to right) Bill Brewer, Rugged Lark and Don Treadway welcome guests to the AQHA reception at the 1989 Volvo World Cup.*

*Rugged* 113 *Lark*

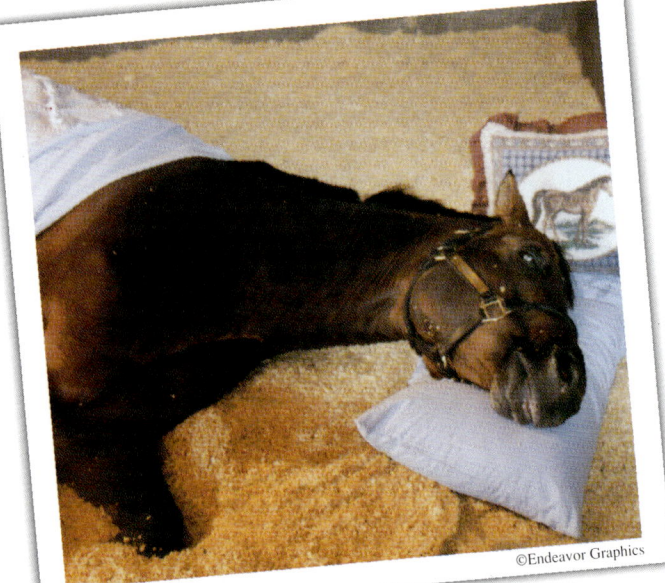

*(top left photo)* Lark and Carol relax after a busy day of Christmas shopping.

*(top right photo)* Sometimes we'd find Lark practicing his bow all by himself.

*(middle left photo)* Lark hated to wake up from <u>this</u> dream.

*(middle right photo)* Lynn and Lark before their last performance together.

*(bottom photo)* Lark and Carol clown around at Bo-Bett.

*Rugged  Lark*

guests in his bowtie and cufflinks.... We'd bought champagne and poured some in Rugged Lark's Superhorse trophy. He liked it better than anyone else!"

"I began drinking champagne with Rugged Lark that evening, and it's now my favorite drink. In fact, I have a list of pleasures I call Bill's Bits on Life, and number ten is 'Drink champagne for no reason at all'...I learned that from Rugged Lark."

How many people can claim they were introduced to their favorite cocktail by a horse?

Another bit of light-hearted horseplay that Carol enjoys has been providing Lark a bag of tricks with which to work his magic connection to others. No one-trick pony, Rugged Lark actively engages in conversation with his head-shaking responses to questions, and shows a noble gratitude at the end of his performances by graciously bowing to his delighted fans. Depending on the occasion, he'll sit up proudly like the overgrown lap dog many claim he is, or sits regally at a table set with candles, crystal and sterling to toast his latest victory. Other times he'll lay down with his head on a pillow and a quilt tucked up under his chin, "dreaming" of his children's future.... The many wonderful gestures that he's learned over the years from trainers Rocky Romano and Butch Campbell endear him to all who see him.

When these tricks of the trade are combined with the first-person commentaries that Carol scripts for each performance, a magical presence is conjured up that naturally leads one to believe that this engaging animal is equal parts human

©D.J. Fitzgerald

*"Depending on the occasion, he'll sit up proudly like the overgrown lap dog many claim he is, or sits regally at a table set with candles, crystal and sterling to toast his latest victory." Here, Lark and Carol drink a toast to another successful year.*

*Some memorable moments from Lark's last performance at the 1997 AQHA World Show.*

*Rugged Lark, Lynn Palm and Carol Harris take a final bow.*

and horse.

As November, 1997, drew near, Carol could hardly believe that the last stop on Rugged Lark's Farewell Tour was approaching. But her creative juices were flowing once again as she conjured up new ideas to thrill the audience for Lark's final performance at the World Show. A couple of months before heading to Oklahoma City another surprise was germinating....

Upon entering the World Show arena, Lynn and Rugged Lark were greeted with the rousing reception of returning heroes. This crowd loved seeing these famous favorites together one last time. The emotion of the moment washed over Lynn.

With all her years of training, practice, competition, exhibitions and professionalism, not much throws Lynn Palm Pittion-Rosillon...not the physical pain of a barn accident, nor the spontaneous surprise of a Superhorse award spectacle, nor the mayhem of a chaotic World Cup Finale, nor the pressure of solo exhibitions at the Olympics.... But even this pro was affected by the emotion of her

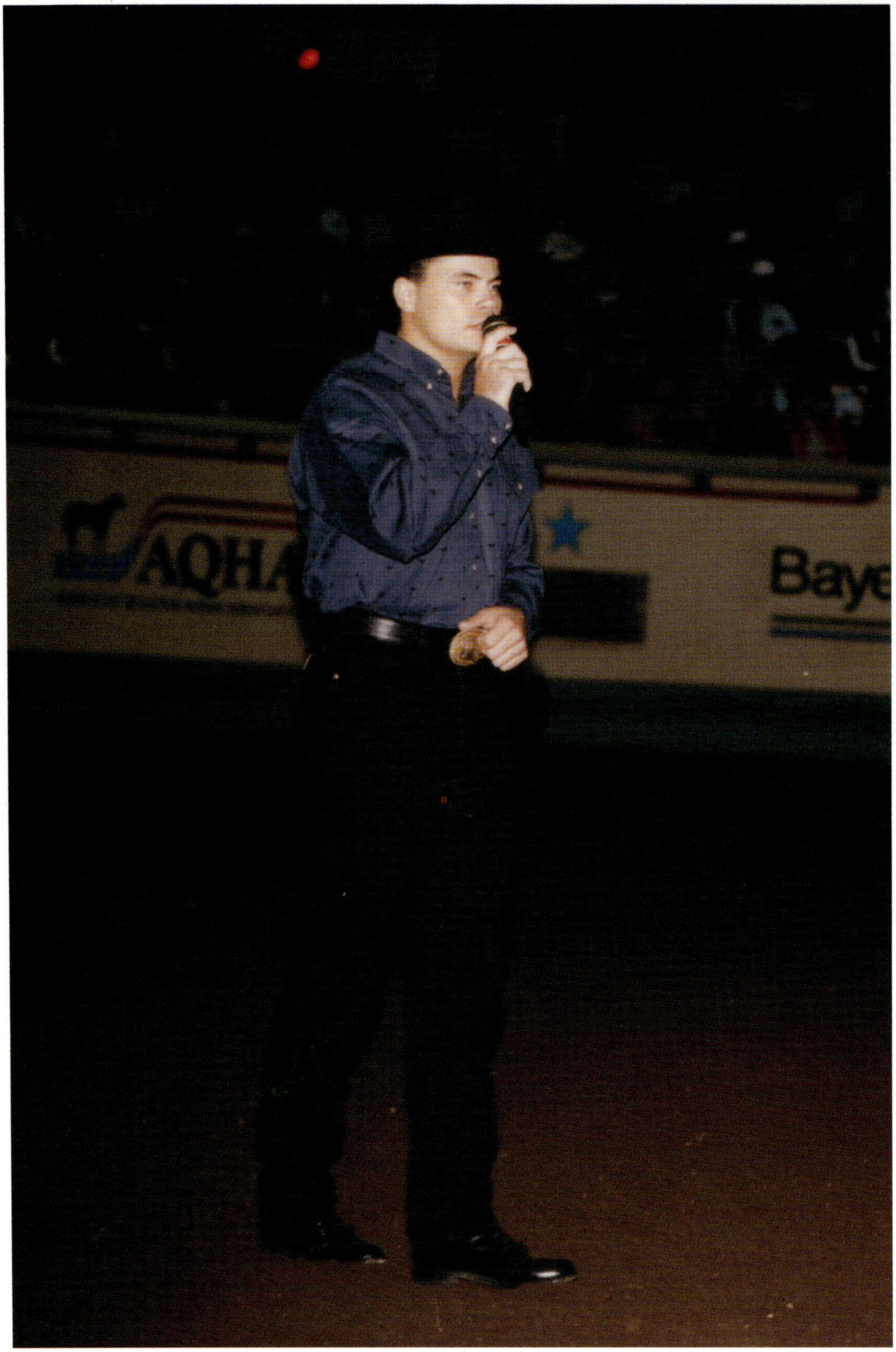

©Sarah Gentry

*Paul Rogers, a talented young singer from Ocala, entertains the crowd with Lark's version of "I Never Met A Man I Didn't Like" during his last performance at the 1997 AQHA World Show.*

*(top photo) AQHA President Ginger Hyland shed a few tears during Lark's last performance.*

*(middle photo) Chris Cox, the mystery cowboy, arrives from "down under" to participate in Lark's finale.*

*(bottom photo) Chris Cox prepares Rugged Lark for his "last ride" exhibition.*

final performance with Rugged Lark.

As the routine unfolded, only Carol, so intimately familiar with each choreographed movement, noticed that Lynn's timing wasn't as crisp as usual: she missed a few of the designated marks, the flying-lead changes were slightly out of sync, and as they approached their second jump she got left behind a little. Small things to be sure, and nothing that anyone except Carol would notice, but they were indications that Lynn was feeling something deeper this time...and it was distracting her normally iron concentration.

To the general observer, however, this fabled equestrian ballet was still beautiful and moving to behold; this dynamic bridleless duet, built on trust, still wowed the thousands of horse lovers present.

A billowing wave of ovation swept through the stands as the pair circled the arena. Lynn exuberantly waved and threw two-handed kisses to the crowd while Lark, with his proud head up, scanned the throngs with a look that said, "Hey, we did good, didn't we!"

After that classic performance, Carol thanked Lynn for all the years of training and performing that she and Lark had enjoyed together. Bayer and the AQHA awarded both women special thank-you photos and presented Rugged Lark with a special tribute poem. Then Lynn took a seat of honor at the side of the arena to watch the rest of the evening's program.

At this point a mischievous twinkle came into Carol's eye as she turned her attention back to the audience and explained, "Lark began his career as a Western Reining horse, so I think it's only fitting that his last ride be in western tack with a cowboy up. So...is there a cowboy here tonight who might like to ride Rugged Lark?" The crowd gasped and hands shot up as uncertain laughter filled the arena. You could never guess what Carol Harris was going to come up with!

Carol swung the microphone around like a pointer

*(top left and bottom photo)*
*Chris Cox and Lark show the crowd that they "ain't seen nothin' yet".*

*(top right photo)*
*"Look ma, no bridle, no nothin!"*

as she surveyed the huge crowd, finally settling on the seating area to her left. "You, in the black hat...come on down!"

The lucky young man wearing a black cowboy hat, checked shirt and blue jeans threaded his way out of the stands to the middle of the arena. Carol shook his hand, then asked his name and where he was from, repeating his answers into the microphone, "He says his name is Chris Cox and he's from Australia."

Again the audience laughed, tickled at the odds of an Australian wrangler being in the right place at the right time to get picked out of the thousands of home-grown American cowhands who'd have given a month's wages to be selected to ride Rugged Lark.

Carol asked, "I assume you've ridden a horse before?"

"A few times," was the noncommittal reply.

"Okay then, you take Lark," she said handing over her Superhorse.

While Lark's tack was being switched, Carol thanked all who had believed in Rugged Lark over the years and helped further his career: the AQHA, Bayer Corporation and the thousands of fans who have made him a superstar. Then she introduced a number of Lark's

*Lark shows everybody what a racing pedigree means.*

trainers: Patty Shortino, Sandy Vaughn, Barbara Williams, Colleen McQuay, Bob Loomis and Butch Campbell; they all took seats in a row of chairs inside the arena next to Lynn.

Carol continued, "As a surprise for everyone, I've asked my friend Paul Rogers, a talented singer from Florida, to help us understand what's in Rugged Lark's mind while he's being ridden by a cowboy." Carol had personalized the lyrics to the Will Rogers Follies' song, 'I Never Met a Man I Didn't Like,' exemplifying Lark's love of people.

When Chris Cox and Rugged Lark arrived back at the in-gate awaiting instructions, Carol looked over and asked, "Are you ready, Lark?" Rugged Lark nodded his head, "Yes" to an appreciative laugh from the audience. When Carol asked Paul if he was ready, he gave an exaggerated bob of his head like Lark had.

On cue, the music swelled and Chris' spurs chinked in rhythm as he walked Lark out, then made his "preflight check" of the saddle, cinch, bridle and the horse's frame of mind.

Meanwhile, Paul delivered Lark's soliloquy: "Howdy! I've done a lot of travelin' in my sixteen years; I've found that all folks want respect just like us horses do. I've even learned how to check out the good folks from the bad ones. It's real easy—the good ones smell better! I always watch how they move, too...comin' at me as well as goin' away. The good folks have a gentle touch that makes us horses lick our lips, relax and understand life's alright. Now it appears I'm about to make a new friend. He sure looks like a cowboy...and yup, he smells okay, too!"

*(top right photo) Bayer Corp. presents Lark with a picture, a poem and some posies.*

*(top left photo) Lark receives a standing ovation for his performance.*

*(bottom left photo) Carol and Lynn say, "Thanks for the memories."*

avoid the thundering stallion. Lark angled across the arena toward the jumps that were still in place on the far side. Carol held her breath as her horse ran hell-bent-for-leather through the darkened arena heading straight for the wooden stanchions. At the last instant, Lark swerved, missing the obstacle and continuing along the arena's far side at even greater speed. Rugged Lark was now racing at a dead run that would make his Thoroughbred ancestors proud!

Carol stood helpless and horrified as Lark exploded past her yet again skidding into a sharp turn at the far corner. Through it all, Paul Rogers continued singing 'I Never Met a Man I Didn't Like' as though this bolting spectacle was all part of the script. As a result, the crowd alternated between gasps of concern and ecstatic cowboy whoops, not really sure if they were witnessing a thrilling equestrian entertainment or an impending disaster. Either way, this was the most exciting exhibition of unadulterated speed they'd ever witnessed at a World Show!

As Lark blew past the line of trainers seated along the near end of the arena a third time, Patty Shortino

*Carley Casper rides Rugged Lark back to the barn after his '97 performance. She thought he was "very funny."*

*"One Moment In Time" we'll never forget.*

*(left to right) Poet, J.D. Hill, Carol, Lark and Bayer Corp. Veterinarian, Craig Barnett.*

*Back at the barn, trainer Mark Stevens and Carol enjoy a moment with Rugged Lark after his final performance.*

recalled, "I was sitting next to Lynn Palm who was saying, 'Well I knew this wouldn't work!' Sandy Vaughn was on my other side saying, 'Shouldn't one of us do something?' And I'm thinking, 'I'm not getting up! If one of us gets up Lark might stop and Chris would be launched....'"

Chris was hanging on with one hand on the cantle in front of him while the other hand gripped the horn behind him. The leather fringe on his chaps and the fabric of his shirt were being whipped by Lark's slipstream like a sail in a gale. As the stallion flew down the arena straightaway, Chris laid down flat, trying once more to reverse his position while traveling at Mach 2. But Lark was simply moving too fast and too hard for Chris to release a handhold long enough to swing his legs over the stud's pounding back. As they approached the turn at the far end of the straightaway, Chris' right leg passed the saddle's mid-point, but he still couldn't release his grip for fear of falling out of control. As his full weight shifted to one side, the saddle slipped and Chris' body began sliding down Lark's flank. Feeling this drastic change in weight, Lark broke to a trot. Chris then let go and hit the dirt...rather gracefully under the circumstances.

Lark jogged straight to Carol who flagged him to a stop and led him back to Chris who was already up and waving to the crowd with his hat signaling that he was alright. When they met, Chris gave Lark a pat, remounted, walked him—freestyle yet again—to the center of the ring, backed and stopped him. Then Chris cued Lark, and as Rugged Lark laid down, Chris stepped deftly out of the saddle to screams of approval. As the audience jumped to their feet, cheering, Chris knelt down, stroked Rugged Lark's neck, gave him a kiss and whispered a sincere apology.... Then Chris stood, nudged Lark up, and both man and mount bowed gallantly to their ecstatic fans....

Since Rugged Lark is celebrated for his renowned restraint and tractable demeanor, those closest to him were shocked and dismayed by his bolting incident and there a number of differing theories as to what happened:

Carol Harris surmises, "Lark doesn't like

discipline and if it's a case of over-discipline...he'll show you somewhere along the way that you shouldn't have done it. The World Show episode was a perfect example. I'd warned Chris to be careful of the spurs because Lark doesn't like them. But he said, 'Carol I've got to use them because this is a hard thing to do and I've got to let him know what I need him to do.'"

"Well, he's the trainer, so I couldn't tell him much—but Lark told him in his own special way."

"Some thought it was part of the act, but while it was happening I was feeling cold-blooded horror because it could have ended terribly.... That was one moment in time I'd love to forget!"

"But on the other hand, it was a lesson to me: that showing-off can lead to being shown-up. This was a case of overkill; we didn't need to do the backwards riding because Lark had already done everything else that nobody could believe: being ridden without any bridle or even a neck-ring and doing lead changes, backing, spins...."

"I had wanted so badly to do this because all of Lark's prior performances had been done in the English discipline. Here we were in Oklahoma, the home of so many great cowboys—including Will Rogers...I wanted Lark's last ride to be Western—and it sure was!"

Chris Cox reports, "Backward riding is such a difficult thing to do, and at the World Show I wasn't able to work with Rugged Lark but one time—at 6:00 in the morning before the performance. He did the whole thing perfectly then, and since it was just a small segment of the piece, I thought he'd be alright.... But this was such a big arena and it was probably too early to do this."

"Halfway through the routine...I don't know what it was, but whenever I squeezed him up into a trot he went into a lope, but I just went with the ride. Carol says it was the spurs, but it wasn't because I didn't have my spurs in him. I know when I use my spurs and when I don't. But I didn't argue with her. From then on I didn't ride him with any spurs because I didn't want to create a fuss."

"At the end," Chris recalls, "the saddle was loose and it slid down the side so I just stepped off. I didn't

*Chad Spring, grandson of Bayer Corp. executive, John Payne, waves to his family.*

*Sparks Rust, left, and Carol Harris, right.*

*Lark visits with good friends (l to r) Evonne Severinson, Barbara Schulte and Rose Tanis*

*1999 AQHA President Ken and Patsy Smith share a moment with Carol and Lark.*

*AQHA President Ginger Hyland presents Carol with a special award honoring Rugged Lark.*

*A bronze by Beverly Zimmer that was presented to Rugged Lark by Linda Wirtz and Jack Van Dell.*

think it was a big deal—everybody else made it into a big deal; I just kind of went with the flow...."

Lynn Palm Pittion-Rossillon concluded that Lark's reaction was a result of Chris overlooking the most important key to controlling Rugged Lark...trust. "For me, watching that run was absolutely horrifying! When it was over, you could see how hard that horse was breathing...he looked like he'd just done the Kentucky Derby! He'd never run like that before, but nobody had felt they had to use spurs with that horse. Obviously Chris didn't trust him, and whether he used the spurs or not, Lark knew they were there. I absolutely think Rugged Lark got him back for not trusting him!"

Marv Jahde of Bayer Corporation offers this simpler assessment shared by many, "A horse is still a horse and sometimes they have a mind of their own.... I think Lark was just trying to say, 'Hey, I'm still in control here!'"

Still others chalk up Lark's response to "showtime syndrome": when the desire to 'get it right' at an important show causes a rider to unconsciously over-cue his mount. This would address Rugged Lark's incidental annoyance and his responding with a lope when Chris felt he was asking for a trot.... It also explains why, as soon as Lark felt Chris going off, he settled down to a trot, and then regained his customary tractability when Chris remounted—facing forward—and asked him to walk, back, halt, lay down, sit-up and bow. Doing all that so cooperatively shows that Lark was still attentive and willing to do what was asked.

In the end however, Rugged Lark is the only one who really knows if it was spurs, overcues, lack of trust, one-ups-manship or simply horseplay as a reminder that he is, after all, a horse, not a human in a really good horse-suit....

Trainer Patty Shortino added, "Most of the crowd thought it was all planned. But once it was over and everyone was okay, we laughed about it more than anything because Carol kept shaking her head, saying, 'Doesn't it just figure...his last go-round!'"

The irony of this latest twist of fate was not lost on Carol as she realized that Rugged Lark's remarkable career had come full circle: it began

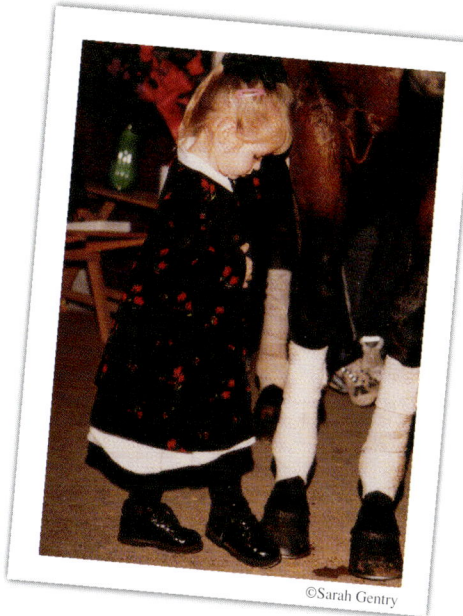

*(top left photo) Carley Casper gives Lark a big hug before comparing her shoe size to his (top right photo).*

*(middle right photo) Lark tells J.D. Blondin and his grandchild 'good night'!*

*(middle left photo) Lark and Carol pose with a young friend.*

*(bottom right photo) More admirers come to give Lark their best wishes.*

with unexpected pilot error and now it had ended with unexpected pilot error.

Although those who commented above knew what had been planned and were disturbed by the unexpected turn of events on Lark's last ride, most of the audience was left with a truly memorable exhibition of pure equine spirit. Jerry Vaughn, a Reining Quarter Horse breeder and California ranch realtor who was in a box at ringside, still remembers the thrill of that ride, "To see that elegant horse running free in that darkened arena was just amazing! I can still picture the whole thing—the memory of it is burned into my mind."

"When I saw that guy get on backwards my first thought was, 'What poor horsemanship.' But then I thought of the entertainment side.... Would you ever ride your horse backwards? ...or without a bridle? Probably not, but that's exactly why the audience loved it. And that's what makes Rugged Lark such a spectacular horse, because how many horses would you even attempt that with? A lot of people there weren't watching with expertise, they were just watching it as entertainment, so it was very spectacular to them."

"There was more speed than I would want to have on a horse running in that arena...especially backwards with no bridle, bit, or reins! I was concerned that Rugged Lark might hit something in the dark, but he's an old veteran...."

"Even the fall didn't look so bad because it was dark and they were at the far end of the arena. I couldn't really tell if he got off or fell off...it just appeared as a not-quite-so-elegant-dismount."

"When he got back on and then laid that horse down the crowd gave him a standing ovation, and he totally deserved it. I thought it was an absolutely great performance and it's something I will always remember...and not as anything flawed," Jerry added. "I remember the standing ovations."

Thus, in spite of his runaway finale, Lark is still the runaway favorite. Nothing can tarnish the living legend of Rugged Lark: actor, athlete, ambassador extraordinaire.... Western or English, rich or poor, young or old, male or female, Quarter Horse enthusiast or not, Rugged Lark wins people over and remains America's most accomplished and beloved Superhorse.

*Can you imagine riding this horse backwards...and without a bridle?*

*Chris gives Lark a kiss and says, "Will you forgive me?"*

# "BORN TO BE A LEGEND"

*by J.D. Hill*

Born to be a legend
One precious moment in time
A trusty steed throughout the years
Like beautiful words that rhyme.

You've made us cry, you've given us laughter
A true friend you've surely been
To Carol your faithful honor
A love that will never end.

At the Olympics you were golden
Bringing crowds to their feet
Grown-ups hold back tears
And young ones think you're neat.

A hero to the children
They dream of you in a lope
You have been an inspiration
To many, a glimpse of hope.

Now on your Farewell Tour
We come to say good-bye
To honor you with cheer
To place your name on high.

Thank you for the memories
And the joy throughout the years
We say good-bye tonight
As we shed our joyous tears.

Your name has been deceiving
Rugged you are not
A horse for all the ages
Out to pasture, but not forgot.

This poem was read and presented to Carol Harris at Lark's farewell performance at Oklahoma City. Her appreciation is forever.

©Cynthia McFarland

*The feeling of confidence I get when I ride Rugged Lark is one that I will never forget. He has a natural born instinct to please, better than any horse I have ever ridden.*

*Chris Cox*

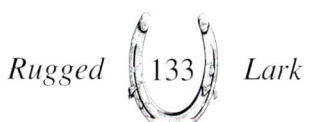

©Sarah Gentry

# Chapter Ten
# Fan Fare

### *"Caramel Corn and Champagne"*

Not many horses have active fan clubs, but as the most recognized Quarter Horse superstar, Rugged Lark has joined the lofty ranks of Secretariat, Roy Rogers' Trigger, and Canada's Big Ben.

"When this horse is mentioned," notes Sue Page, "it's like talking about Michael Jordan—everybody knows Rugged Lark."

Patty Shortino agrees, recalling the time Lark was at her barn for a training session, "Everyone at the barn knew who Rugged Lark was, so all the kids wanted to see him and pet him. It was like hosting a rock star!"

"He has such a friendly personality that everybody takes to...and he pretty much takes to everybody. Most horses couldn't put up with what he's had in his life—all kinds of people and goings on. But it never bothered Lark, actually, it always seemed like he enjoyed it."

That natural charisma, plus the fact that he started winning "right out of the chute" and continued piling honor upon honor throughout his career, has also made Rugged Lark a media darling. Extensive coverage of show triumphs, command performances and exciting exhibitions by all the major equestrian communication venues have earned him a broad following in competitive, entertainment, and down-home circles.

When one magazine reported that Lark's favorite food wasn't carrots, apples, or sweet feed but rather Fiddle Faddle®, cartons of the caramel corn snack began flooding into Bo-Bett from tickled fans all over the country.

"It seems Carol knew from the very beginning that this was a special horse," reports Colleen McQuay,

*Carol, Sue Page and Roger Chappell relax for a moment at the Special Olympics.*

*(top photo)*
*Lark directs his attention to his favorite treat, Fiddle-Faddle®.*

*(bottom photo)*
*Wendy and Carol read the poems and songs, accompanied by numerous pictures, written for Lark at the 1997 AQHA World Show.*

"because she provided a lot of things to allow him to be special. When Rugged Lark came to my place to train for awhile, a groom came and stayed with him to give Lark his early morning hand-walk and make sure he wasn't left tied in cross-ties or tied in the stall."

"I loved that this horse was treated that way...as such an individual, because most of the time in this business, you get pushed and calendared and scheduled to death and don't get the opportunity to do what you'd like for each animal. It was fun for me to see a horse treated so special...and it made me feel special to be able to ride him."

"Of course when I rode Rugged Lark he was already a well-known, very well-respected horse, but nowhere near as popular and famous as he is today. That was just the beginning...I knew I had a good horse and a great opportunity," Colleen recalls, "but I had no idea that it would go down in history!"

But down in history it went as Rugged Lark's career was chronicled, not only by the industry's print media, but by newspapers and television as well, with featured appearances on 'America's Horse', 'In the Company of Animals', and most recently, 'Animal Planet'.

As a result of this mass exposure, life for Carol Harris changed markedly. Suddenly she's in charge of a superstar with groupies! Lark's devoted fans send him letters, poems, drawings, photos, and songs in addition to an on-going supply of Fiddle Faddle®.

Now a familiar face as Rugged Lark's "mother," people recognize Carol and often greet her on sight. "I can't even get through the Atlanta Airport without two or three people asking, 'How's Rugged Lark?' "

And when we're on the road, I'll hear, 'Hey, Mrs. Lark!'...it's like traveling with Elvis!

"And people phone us from the highway, 'We're coming through your area, can we stop by?' There's no way I can say no."

"We also get busloads visiting the farm. One day three buses arrived at once and I about died! There were so many people I couldn't talk to them because I didn't have a bullhorn; but they were wonderful.... I try to let all of them come even if it's way after we've closed because I know what it would mean to me."

"To have a horse like this...it would be a shame not to share him. Plus, it's fun because people demand so little and are so interested in this kind of life. It makes me remember myself as a child—horses were all I thought about. But I never thought I'd have anything like this...never in a million years!"

*(top photo) Lark is greeted by some of three busloads of visitors to Bo-Bett Farm.*

*(bottom photo) Carol Harris welcomes the visitors to the farm.*

As was Carol, there are literally millions of horse-crazy kids who dream of owning a horse like Rugged Lark. The Breyer model of Lark gives them a tangible facsimile to claim until their real dreamhorse comes along. Carol and Lynn have signed thousands of these toy horses over the years turning them into meaningful mementos and valuable collectibles.

"At a recent trade show in Maryland," says Lynn Palm, "I saw some young girls with Rugged Lark models and said, 'You're holding my boyfriend.' One of them responded, 'Rugged Lark's better than a boyfriend.'"

"Come to think of it," laughs Lynn, "Lark's so honest and happy all the time, she has a point!"

The younger set weren't the only ones falling in love with Rugged Lark. During the 1996 Farewell Tour, Bayer's Marv Jahde noticed an exceptional reaction from fans.

*Hagen Baker proudly shows Carol his Breyer model of Rugged Lark.*

"There is truly a special bond between people and this horse. The respect and the love people showed for Lark was absolutely phenomenal to see.

"Lark always put his best foot forward and really, really enjoyed what he was doing. You could see that in the way he went through the whole program with a kind of smile on his face. It's almost like he knew when it was his time to get out there and perform. He's really got a presence that the audience connects to very quickly," Marv recalls. "It was fun to watch."

Artist Debbie Fitzgerald agrees, adding, "When you watch Rugged Lark perform, you see a horse that loves his work. Just before he goes out to do a performance, Rugged Lark stands soaking up the atmosphere of the crowd and you can see that he loves going out there and performing. Most horses are obedient and will do it; they know what they're supposed to do and resign themselves to it, but Lark just eats it up!"

Even a veteran who's witnessed literally thousands of equine exhibitions and competitions is impressed by Rugged Lark. As Keith Bradley reports, "I've had the pleasure of announcing a number of Lynn and Lark's performances, and each time it's such a delight to watch him come out: his head's up, he's paying attention and he's ready for business. He goes around the pen in a nice, easy lope. He's

*Rugged Lark loves his young fans, he always greets them with his ears forward.*

always presented himself beautifully—like one of the queen's guards—very, very proper. He looks good and shows good."

Presence, personality and presentation will certainly get an animal noticed, but to gain the kind of following Rugged Lark has, the horse must perform exceptionally as well.

"Rugged Lark converts people with his elegance," says Butch Campbell, "the way he strides converts you."

"But the best thing is the way Carol, Mike and Lynn brought him up as far as trust with the horse. I'm glad they saw this in him. Carol is a very good horsewoman and loves the mind of the horse. All you have to do is look in Lark's eyes—he's just the sweetest, well-mannered, personable horse there probably is...and he converts you."

Another star quality that Lark possesses is his natural sense of showmanship which results in rave reviews throughout the horse community. Leslie Groves, AQHA liaison for Rugged Lark's Farewell Tour explains, "One of my major complaints about a horse show is it's not a show. Spectators are the very last consideration at horse events, and with no showmanship, it's not much fun to watch. Rugged Lark is a performance horse, and with his charisma and tricks there's showmanship about him. Watching Rugged Lark compete or perform is always entertainment."

Trainer Chris Cox concurs, "The show industry has made our horses so mechanical...we've over-trained them to the point that they don't have any way of responding or bringing out their own personality. They have to fit a judge's template, so they're trained the same and they lose all that personality that actually makes a horse unique."

"A big part of Rugged Lark's popularity comes from his personality and how he responds to people—he plays crowds. He's like a little show-off, he'll perk up and look, or yawn and respond in all sorts of ways that are cute. He actually performs better in front of crowds because he displays his character in a way that people really understand...kind of like a movie star who gets in front of the spotlight. He certainly knows that the people are there to see him."

"And when you perform with him, he'll look at everybody in the stands and check them out...people love that. He comes so alive and shows off—not prancing around, but with cuteness, his eye appeal towards crowds. This is what we're all trying to get our horses to be like."

Veterinarian, Dr. G. Marvin Beeman adds another point about eye appeal, "This horse has such attraction because of his beauty and the way Lynn presented him—she's attractive, he's attractive.... And I never saw Rugged Lark not do well every time he was asked to do something. There aren't very many horses capable of doing that. That's why he's got such a fan club."

Obviously there are a number of factors that turn horse lovers into Rugged Lark fans. Many cite Lark's charismatic ability to relate to people, noting that during a performance, Rugged Lark seems to give to, and connect with spectators as surely as he does with his rider. As a result, watching Lark is a uniquely personal affair. There may be thousands in the stands, but Rugged Lark makes everyone in the crowd feel like he appreciates each of them as much as they do him. That personal connection and mutual admiration binds the audience to him.

Breeder and auctioneer Blair Folck witnessed this phenomenon when Lynn and Lark were performing

*Photographer-Journalist Leslie Groves and a young lady have a long conversation with "you know who"!*

during the 1996 Olympic trials at Gladstone. "There were two show rings working at the time: one in which the Olympic tryouts were being held, but there wasn't anyone watching that—they were all watching Rugged Lark in the other ring and giving him standing ovations."

The crowning source of Lark's attraction lies in his confidence and pride. As AQHA Vice President, Bill Brewer observes, "Rugged Lark knows better than all of us who he is, and he's really proud of who he is...people respond to that."

Personality, presence, presentation, performance and pride add up to a magical love-potion that attracts fans to Rugged Lark like bees to honey. And not just diehard horse fans. As Keith Bradley's secretary, Peggy Brigham is exposed to the business of horses, yet had only a passing interest in the animals themselves—until she saw Rugged Lark.

*Carol Harris, Leslie Baker, & Marv Jahde at Equitana USA in 1997.*

As Peggy explains, "I don't know anything about horses except that they've got four legs and they're beautiful animals. The first time I saw Rugged Lark perform I got a lump in my throat because it was such an awesome experience for me."

"I'd seen other horses perform, but I'd never seen a horse with as much charisma, magnitude, and forcefulness as this horse. He was so gentle and so magnificent, I just couldn't get enough of him. When I got the opportunity to meet Lynn and Carol, Carol said, 'You can pet him if you want to.'"

"I asked, 'Are you sure?'"

"'Oh, you bet you can!' She was very warm and hospitable, so I got to pet Rugged Lark and get closer to him...WOW! It was really something! I couldn't believe I actually got to pet this superstar."

"During my childhood I had cats and dogs, but I never had an animal of that magnitude, that big. So when I was able to go up to this horse and pet it and he was so gentle and trusting...that really excited me! He wasn't going to hurt me. Here we were one-on-one...friends."

"I have his Breyer statue right on top of my desk, so I get to see Rugged Lark everyday," says Peggy. "And Carol was so nice that I got to have my picture taken with her and Lark and Mr. Bradley. I'll treasure that forever."

When Peggy first saw Rugged Lark perform, she discovered the same love-at-first-sight thrill one feels when witnessing an exquisite ballet performance for the first time. One needn't study—or even enjoy—ballet to be wowed by the grace, athleticism, and charisma of a Barishnikov, then fall in love with the spirit behind that ability.

Discovering such a spirit, as Peggy did in Lark, and then being allowed to associate with it is an intoxicating thrill. Thus, another aspect of Rugged Lark's special allure is found in Carol's trusting him

*Gordon Smith, of Oregon, wears his Rugged Lark cap to celebrate his election to the US Senate. "This fancy stallion is everyone's buddy."*

to be accessible. By allowing such friendly access to her superstar, Carol's added another memorable perk to Rugged Lark's fan club."

"At the All American Quarter Horse Congress there'd always be people five or six deep around Rugged Lark's stall on Stallion Avenue," Nancy Folck reports. "Carol would literally leave the stall door open and Lark would just stand there as people trooped in, petted and fussed over him, then trooped out. You wouldn't normally do that with a stallion!"

But this is no fancy, high-strung stallion that has to be penned and can't be touched. This fancy stallion is everyone's buddy.

One of Lark's regular visitors was journalist and photographer, Leslie Groves. "Whenever Lark was at the World Show," Leslie notes, "I'd stop at this one truckstop on the way to buy Lark his Fiddle Faddle®. The first few years he was there, people would walk past his stall and not know who he was because he's just a bay horse until he starts being 'Rugged Lark'."

"Sometimes when nobody was around, I'd sit in the corner of his stall playing 'yawny-yawny' (getting him to yawn on cue) and we'd share a box of Fiddle Faddle® and just kind of hang out."

"There are a lot of horses that I admire," Leslie continues, "and there were probably a thousand horses on the World Show grounds at any given time, but Lark's the only one that it would ever cross my mind to prepare for our visit. He's the only one that I feel like, 'I'm going to get to see my friends at the World Show: so and so, and so and so, and Rugged Lark.'"

"A while ago I was out with friends when someone asked, 'If you were to plan a fantasy dinner party with anyone in the world, who would you invite?' I put Rugged Lark on my list because he's fun, everyone's happy to see him, and he looks great in black tie."

Leslie Groves isn't the only one who made plans for Rugged Lark visits. As AQHA Coordinator Leslie Baker recalled, "When the Farewell Tour was at Equitana in 1997, we were all in the Trade Show when a young couple arrived wearing matching Rugged Lark tee-shirts. They told us they'd just gotten married and were honeymooning at Equitana so they could see Rugged Lark perform. They'd sought him out and were so excited to be able to pet him and have their picture taken with him. That was neat."

Keith Bradley understood their thinking Rugged Lark was special enough to be a honeymoon destination. "Lark's a real fun horse to be around. Some of the things Carol's done with him...you know darn well she's spoiled him. Spoiled him, BUT he still has manners and that's the important part."

Those manners include "asking for snacks" as Nancy Folck reports, "On Stallion Avenue, whenever Lark wanted some Fiddle Faddle®, he'd bang on his stall wall and Carol would say, 'Okay, Lark' and she'd get him some—like a mother with a little kid."

At times, however, it wasn't really clear who had control of Lark's Fiddle Faddle® habit, as Debbie Fitzgerald observed, "Carol's got this odd dichotomy about her: she's very particular about how Lark is handled, but she'll trot him into her office, or take him to a party on a whim...."

"There must have been seventy-five people partying in the barn at Christmas when Carol brought that stallion out of the stall with no halter on and proceeded to lead him around with Fiddle Faddle®! Carol was a little looped at that point and Lark knew—he knew—he had her, so he kept nudging her for more...soon Fiddle Faddle®'s flying all over the place."

"I remember thinking this could get out of hand real quick, so I asked Wendy, 'Don't you think it's about time to put him up?'"

"'In a minute....'"

"He was fine the whole time," Debbie concedes. "A total gentleman! Any other horse would have said, 'Oh, boy!' and that would be it...but Lark has this incredible self-restraint about him. He's probably the smartest horse I've ever met."

Taking advantage of Rugged Lark's intelligence and incorporating his light-hearted tricks such as nodding "Yes, I'm ready" at the World Show and bowing, personalize his shows and daily routine, endearing him to friends and fans alike.

"It's those personal touches that people appreciate," says Carol. "They can get to Lark and touch him. They don't have to stand outside a paddock and look in at him. They can go on in if they want, get close and have their picture taken."

"I feel that I owe this to the people that love him. These are the people who have cried at his performances. They come up to you with tears streaming down their face...."

"I overheard one man talking to his wife on a telephone after one of Lark's shows saying, 'Mary, I saw the god-damndest thing today. You should have been here! This horse...I was bawlin' like a baby!'"

"The public feels like he's their horse," Carol explains. "Even little kids have been able to see this horse, touch the horse, pet the horse, sit on the horse—things that don't ordinarily go along with a famous horse."

Leslie Groves relates a story that took place at one of Rugged Lark's shows in 1996, "After the performance, I saw Terry Bradshaw [Pittsburgh Steelers Superbowl quarterback and television sports commentator] with his daughters and asked, "Are you a Rugged Lark fan?"

"'My daughters eat, breathe and sleep Rugged Lark,' he said. 'They want to go see him.'"

"So I took them over and Carol let the girls get

*(top photo) Super Bowl Quarterback, Terry Bradshaw, and daughters, Erin and Rachel, congratulate Rugged Lark, Carol and Lynn after their dramatic performance.*

*(bottom photo) Rugged Lark is swarmed by approximately 100 children outside of his stall on Stallion Avenue at the 1995 All American Quarter Horse Congress.*

*(top photo)* Don Treadway, Carol Harris, and Marv Jahde at Equitana USA in 1997.

*(bottom photo)* Carol signs Lark's Breyer model and video for fans in Oklahoma City.

on Lark while I snapped a photo with Terry's instamatic camera, which wasn't all that easy since there was just a sea of people."

"I've seen this horse with literally a hundred people crowded around him," Leslie notes. "You can imagine what having a crowd of people all around you means to a prey animal. When people [predators] are directly behind or surrounding a prey animal, it usually feels very vulnerable and nervous. For a horse to overcome the instinct to wheel around or kick out, it has to have a lot of confidence that nothing is going to happen to it. Lark's had so many opportunities to strike out, yet he never has."

Bayer Corporation's Marv Jahde saw that this aspect of Rugged Lark magic impressed spectators during the Farewell Tour. "Many people have a perception of stallions being aggressive, ready to fight or kill type of thing. Yet here you have a sixteen-year-old stallion interacting with his owner, trainers, the general public and little kids in crowded, noisy, busy situations with no restraints. Knowing what this horse could do, people wonder how can this be? Then they see the strong trust and confidence between Carol and Lark. They see that, connect with it, are in awe of it, and want to be part of it some how, some way...."

Tour coordinator and horsewoman, Leslie Baker was equally impressed and comments, "Personally, I don't think many people should own stallions because most require expert handling, but we all want to believe in the myth of owning a stallion and all that goes with that.... This makes Lark even more special—the fact that as a stallion he's a complete horse."

And that's the wonder of Rugged Lark. Rugged Lark is our mythical stallion in the flesh, giving us the opportunity to see, to touch and to love the inspiring power and beauty of a complete horse. His incredibly dependable nature allows people to interact with him on an unprecedented level. Most famous horses are kept at a liability-safe distance from admirers. Fences and stall bars are always there between horse and human. You may look, but

*Rugged Lark, Lynn Palm and Carol perform at the Ocala Shrine Rodeo.*

don't touch!

But Rugged Lark needs no barriers, no separation—you can pat him, hug him, get on him, take a souvenir hair from his tail.... This wins Rugged Lark fans, yet it's not promotion. It's only possible due to Lark's exceptional temperament coupled with Carol's sincere desire to share the experience of her wonderful horse. Carol genuinely believes that Lark is America's horse on a level that is so incredibly generous.

"Carol's had a lot of success and a lot of fun with Rugged Lark and wants everybody else to enjoy the success and the fun, too," says Patty Shortino. "She not only took Lark to the National Horse Show and the Olympics, she also did local shows, so local people got to see him and enjoy him."

Leslie Baker adds, "One thing I'm reminded of is how gracious Carol was to share Rugged Lark on the Farewell Tour. His value as a sire and an athlete was already well-established. He'd made many appearances and had a huge fan following, so there wasn't an overwhelming need for Carol to take Lark on that tour and take on all that extra work."

"Due to my involvement in the tour, I got to see things that others didn't see—like Carol signing autographs for hours on end because she is really Rugged Lark's voice. She signed autographs for children, adults, grandparents, people with lots of money, people with little money...people from all walks of life. There wasn't anyone who came up to talk to Carol about Rugged Lark that she did not try to make a minute for. And that's hard to do. People only got to see their minute of it, but I got to see the hours of it."

One such signature story occurred when Rugged Lark was exhibiting in Kentucky. Carol was busy

Rugged 146 Lark

signing autographs for a long line of people. At one point, she looked up and saw Bob Baffert, the famous Thoroughbred racing trainer of Kentucky Derby winner Silver Charm, standing in line. Laughing, he jumped the line and strode up to Carol saying, "Hey, lady, what would it take to get a picture of this bay S.O.B.?" He then walked over, opened Lark's stall door and the cameras started flashing! Before long, he and Rugged Lark were joined by Bob's friend, Carl Nafzger, renowned trainer of racing great, Unbridled.

Another celebrity encounter included William Shatner, the movie actor who's involved with Reining horses and Saddlebreds. After watching Rugged Lark's performances at the National Horse Show at New Jersey's Meadowlands, he stopped Carol in the lobby of their hotel and said, "I really like your horse." Then he offered magnanimously, "If you bring him out to California, I could probably get him booked to a lot of good mares."

Carol thanked him and laughed, "But what would I do with my mares if I sent him to California?"

Shatner answered, "Oh, that's easy...just send them out with him!"

"Thank you very much," she replied, "but I think I'd better keep him home."

Journalist Leslie Groves tells of another who appreciated sharing a few minutes of Carol's time, "My parents divorced when I was eight, and as an only child, my mom and I were very, very close. Mom always came to the World Show to see me. After Rugged Lark started appearing she'd come and bring some friends who worked at the savings

*(opposite page) Local people enjoy a performance by Lark and Chris Cox at Golden Hills Country Club in Ocala, Florida.*

*(top photo) Carol signs autographs in Oklahoma City.*

*(middle photo) Famous thoroughbred trainer, Bob Baffert, meets Rugged Lark at Equitana USA.*

*(bottom photo) Bob Baffert introduces Lark to renowned trainer and friend, Carl Nafzger.*

*In North Carolina at the Special Olympics we found Special kids love a special horse.*

and loan with her to watch his performances."

"Mom would see industry pictures in the equestrian magazines she read so she could pick people out of the crowd at the World Show. I got so tickled at the Reining Futurity one year when she nudged me and said, 'Look, that's Bob Loomis sitting in front of us.'"

"I asked, 'When did you meet him?'"

"'I've never met him, I've just seen his picture in the magazines....'"

"One time when we were in the Trade Show, I saw Carol and wanted to introduce her to Mom. At the time, my mother was terminally ill with cancer although she was still getting around pretty well."

"When I introduced them, Carol hugged Mom like she'd known her all of her life, then looked her in the eye and said, 'Your daughter is so special to us.' Carol talked with her for awhile and that just meant the world to Mom. For her it was a kind of brush with celebrity...and Carol doesn't even realize that she has that affect on people."

"I have the utmost respect for Carol Harris, and I love her with every part of me because she's been special to me in ways she doesn't even know."

Movie star, royalty, sports celebrity, average Joe or Jane, Carol Harris appreciates and treats everyone with the same genuine warmth and consideration. As Keith Bradley observes, "Carol shares so very, very much with so many people. She doesn't seem to worry whether they've got ten cents in their pocket or ten million, they're all alike to Carol and she treats them alike."

That egalitarian attitude applies to Rugged Lark as well. He may be an international celebrity, but Carol doesn't cater to stardom as Leslie Baker reports, "One thing I appreciate is that even though

Rugged Lark's a very special horse with superstar status there's no pretense surrounding him. So often nowadays you hear about movie or rock stars who demand exotic foods or a certain color dressing room. As an industry superstar, you might expect that Rugged Lark would roll up in a huge, shiny van and have the red carpet rolled out everywhere during his tour. That's not how it was...we just tried to get him a secure, safe place, not because he's this big celebrity, but because that's what you need to do for your horse."

"During that year of his Farewell Tour, I realized that Rugged Lark represents qualities that I value in life: to be a hard worker, to be honest, and to be who I am without pretense...I try to have that in my life."

Not only did Rugged Lark not arrive in a fancy van, this valuable stud traveled America's highways, byways, and freeways with no insurance!

"I hauled this horse all over the country to all those shows without an ounce of insurance on him," says Carol. "I wouldn't have even known what to put on him! I always figured the best insurance is to take extra good care of him. Don't let other people haul him, we'll do it ourselves; that way if I go, he goes...."

And America wasn't the only country interested in hosting Rugged Lark. "We received lots of invitations to exhibit in many places, such as Italy and Sweden," notes Carol. "But as Lark's popularity grew, it got to where some people would get a little upset if I couldn't accept. That's part of the reason I retired him."

One of the invitations Carol couldn't resist, however, was for the 1999 Special Olympics in Raleigh, North Carolina. This was a wonderful opportunity to introduce the magic of Rugged Lark to a whole new group of children. Carol's excitement was only matched by her friend Don Treadway's concern. As the AQHA's Public Relations Director, it was his responsibility to make sure everything went smoothly.

*(top photo) The crowds get a glimpse of Rugged Lark at the Special Olympics.*

*(middle photo) Maria Shriver and her children visit with Chris and Rugged Lark.*

*(bottom photo) It looks like everybody's having a great time in North Carolina. Don Treadway and Rugged Lark visit with Becky Newell, editor of America's Horse.*

*Rugged* 149 *Lark*

*At the Special Olympics, Rugged Lark is surrounded by fans and makes another special friend.*

Although Lark's safety record in groups was unblemished, Don was concerned that a crowd of children encumbered with crutches, braces and wheelchairs might make even steady Rugged Lark anxious.

And Carol admits candidly, "Lark's a very cool cat—whatever happens he takes it—crowds don't bother him, cattle don't bother him, dogs don't bother him.... But I don't trust any horse implicitly—not even Lark."

"I remember once at the Congress when he was out in front of his stall...I don't know whether there was another stud saying something to him or what, but I could tell he was getting pissed. Most times he'd stand out there and have photo shoots surrounded by people, no problem...but I watch him like a hawk. I watch the eye—the eye tells it all."

"That time I could tell something was bothering him, so I just put him up, saying, 'Lark's tired, he's got to go back to bed.'"

Both Carol and Don realized if Rugged Lark got excited in a crowd of handicapped youngsters with all their various prosthetic hardware, an incident could rapidly escalate to disaster because these kids couldn't get out of his way quickly or easily.

"I know I've given Don Treadway heart attacks," Carol admits. "Like at the Special Olympics when he was hosting an AQHA ice cream party for contestants and their families and someone came up and said, 'Carol, do you know there are some kids in the stall with Rugged Lark?'"

"Hearing that, Don turned white, 'What?!' he said."

"We looked, and sure enough, there were three kids in with Lark. Two alongside of him and one right under his belly behind his front legs! They were just hanging out, having a talk while he ate his hay. I could tell he was fine, but poor Don's head immediately filled with visions of lawsuits."

Don Treadway's not the only one whose heart has missed a beat or two due to the potential for disaster. Butch Campbell relates this story from Gladstone, "Carol was busy talking, so someone else was holding Rugged Lark. When I turned and looked, there was a whole crowd of people around Rugged Lark. I could not believe what I was seeing: kids sitting on the ground by his hind legs, his front legs...all over! I was scared to death!"

"I called Carol's attention to it, and she looked over to see Lark standing there like, 'ho hum,' and said, 'He's okay.'"

"And you know what? That horse just loved it!"

*Mr. & Mrs. Jim Shoemake help Carol and Lark at the Special Olympics.*

"That is very unusual for a stallion to be like that," states Butch. "I don't know another stallion that I would trust in that way."

But throughout his career, even with all his high-profile venues, Carol's prize stallion has always been gentle with people, never hurting anyone through malice or mishap. This is one of the many remarkable attributes of Rugged Lark that Chris Cox appreciates the most. "For a stallion, Lark was always so consistent, so together all the time. I have a friend who said, 'Boy, I wish I had that horse's blood pressure!'"

A seasoned horseman, even Chris was amazed by Rugged Lark's behavior at the Special Olympics. He rode Lark at that event and was knocked out by his partner's conduct around the children there. "I was standing with Lark when a handicapped child buzzed up to us in a motorized wheelchair. That would have set off a lot of horses, but Lark didn't even flinch. He laid his head on that little boy's shoulder and nuzzled his ear...."

"The affection that horse showed! I know he loves children, but the way he reacted to those handicapped kids was unbelievable."

Carol's friend, Nancy Folck, also finds Lark's compassion remarkable, "Rugged Lark has many human-like qualities and is able to communicate with people through his

*(top photo) Lark lays down for Lynn Palm and has his picture taken with some fans.*

*(bottom photo) Bob and Judy Standish were responsible for Rugged Lark's many invitations to perform at the Festival of Champions in Gladstone, New Jersey.*

intelligence and gifted ability. He seems to love people and enjoys pleasing them. And in return, people love him—especially the children."

USET's Bob Standish finds support for Nancy's observation right in his own family. "It's quite obvious whenever you see Rugged Lark at one of his competitions that he loves people. He just seems to revel in the fact that he has this crowd of admirers constantly around him. I know my daughter, for one, is one of his great admirers. Kate's a senior in college now, but one of her greatest treasures is a picture of herself and Lark autographed by Carol."

Lynn Palm is very familiar with the love young ones feel for Rugged Lark, "Little kids absolutely idolize this horse. During the Farewell Tour at the Congress, one little girl came up to me crying and obviously upset. When I asked her what was the matter, she said, 'Does this mean I won't see Rugged Lark any more?'"

It's always sad whenever beloved stars begin to fade from our lives. So take a moment to reflect on your all-time favorite superstar. Now imagine your star has a generous personality that makes you feel like he performs just for you at his shows. Imagine further that when you show up backstage for a visit, he's genuinely happy to see you. Now shed all disbelief and picture this same superstar welcoming you with a deferential bow into his home for a chat, a bite to eat, and a drink...say, caramel corn and champagne?

This is the Rugged Lark experience...no wonder he has a fan club! This horse has a huge, devoted following because he's earned the love, trust and respect of millions. Rugged Lark is truly America's Superhorse.

*(opposite page)*
*Total trust and mutual admiration between a gentleman and a baby.*

## Chapter Eleven
# An Exaltation of Larks
### "Superhorse Legacy"

In the context of Rugged Lark, this chapter heading has an interesting double meaning with the word "exaltation" referring to the praising of an influential figure, and the entire phrase used as an idiom to describe a flight of small birds. Thus, "an exaltation of larks" brings to mind the honoring of the champion himself, as well as the flock of talented young Larks on flights of excellence of their own.

As we've seen, Rugged Lark's record and ambassadorial efforts earned him consistent exaltation from all corners of the horse industry, like this declaration from former AQHA President Jim Barton, "The combination of Rugged Lark and Carol—a Superhorse and a super person—they're the best ambassadors you could ever send anywhere."

And thoughtful assessments such as Marv Jahde's noting that the AQHA and Bayer found a winning formula when they selected Rugged Lark to represent the breed: "Bayer is the oldest corporate sponsor of the AQHA, and Rugged Lark's Tour was one of Bayer's most successful sponsorship activities with AQHA. It was a big project that had very positive impacts:"

"Number one, it showcased Quarter Horse versatility with the horse that competed in multiple disciplines, won and became Superhorse two times. That's a real positive thing."

"Second, from a horse industry standpoint, it brought people to events that might not have come without the draw of Rugged Lark. I've never before seen people give the overwhelming attention they gave this horse.

*(opposite page)*
*A portrait of Rugged Lark by Carol Roark*

*(right photo)*
*Two Superhorses, "One For the Record" and "Rugged Lark" produced this super filly. Her name is "That's A Record" & she is owned by the Kaplow family.*

*Rugged Lark and Lynn Palm sail over the Bayer jump at the Congress.*

©Harold Campton

Lark really attracted a crowd wherever he went."

"Thirdly, from Bayer's standpoint, the Farewell Tour brought a tremendous amount of very positive exposure, bringing the name 'Bayer' in front of a lot of people. That really enhanced Bayer's leadership position in the horse industry, so we at Bayer definitely believe it was worthwhile."

While a horse of Rugged Lark's caliber is obviously a valuable boon to the business of horses, breeder and broker Nancy Folck reflects on the more human rewards of Lark's influence, "There are many other horses that can do some of the same things that Rugged Lark does, but he has a special charisma and a kindness that serves as a reminder that we all should show love and kindness to one another. He's a role model we want to duplicate, and fortunately, he is passing much of his personality and ability on to his babies. What a wonderful world this would be if we all followed this example."

Leslie Baker brings up yet another positive benefit of Rugged Lark's career—uniting the horse community by winning fans across the board. "The horse world can be very divided by discipline, by breed, by sport, by all kinds of things.... I don't think that's the way we should be, but we are."

"As a proven champion in the show arena, Rugged Lark possesses enough athleticism, enough versatility and enough charisma that people who are fans of different disciplines and breeds respect him and could imagine him in other roles. They could imagine him—or his get—as a rope horse, a hunter, a trusted trail horse, and I think that's why he's reached across those barriers."

A promotional hero, Rugged Lark has also been instrumental in inspiring newcomers to get involved in equestrian sports and pastimes, as Leslie Baker notes, "It's important that we seek out and even cultivate leaders—human and horse—for the AQHA and the Quarter Horse industry as a whole. We've made heroes of horses that have won at the Olympics and riders who have been at the top of their game for many years. That's important because it gives people something to shoot for."

"Heroes in the horse industry still tend to be very approachable compared to other sports or entertainment heroes, and that reaches out to young people."

"It may have to wait a few years, but people find that their childhood dream of having a horse can come true," Leslie continues. "There aren't a lot of sports that you can participate in throughout life, but like golfing, you can ride horses for many, many years. So Lark's example also reaches out to people who are forty or fifty, and on up the scale as older people are getting horses for the first time."

Breeder Don McDuffee also appreciates Lark's wide appeal, "Rugged Lark's done more to promote Quarter Horses than any other horse in history. He wins people over in huge groups regardless of their discipline. When he performs, it's standing room only."

However, making his mark in competition or exhibition is just the start for a stallion. In order to be truly great, a stallion must make his mark in breeding as well.

A supporter of working with Mother Nature, Carol's breeding program was traditionally live-cover. As Don McDuffee relates, "Last year, Carol asked us to help her start an A-I [artificial insemination] program with Rugged Lark. Since Lark had no experience being collected on a phantom, or breeding dummy, Carol had some concerns, 'I'm not sure at his age [eighteen] that he'll even accept that.'"

"But I told her, 'Carol, this horse is so smart, it won't take long.'"

"We made a deal that as soon as we had a mare in heat, we'd run a test on him: get him collected, then see how well the semen would

*Don and Brenda McDuffee with Rugged Lark. "He is one the easiest horses we have ever worked with," Don says.*

*Mike Corrington broke and trained Mr. Feelin' Good, another Bo-Bett Hall of Fame Reining Horse.*

cool and how long it would last in an equitainer and a bioflite container.

"When we had a mare in heat, I called and Carol brought Lark over."

"That first time, we introduced him to the breeding mount, got him collected and back in the trailer...in about ten minutes! This horse is very, very intelligent."

"The semen tested and shipped very well and last year we did all the breeding and collecting on Rugged Lark and had a very successful season shipping to every part of the country."

Don's wife and business partner, Brenda McDuffee was also impressed by this stud. "Soon after we started working with Rugged Lark, another breeder was visiting and I said, 'You'll be amazed to watch this horse collect because he's so well-mannered.'"

"The mares were in the stocks and Lark knew what he was there to do.... Usually by that time most stallions are straining at the bit to get to the good part, but Lark was so quiet standing there letting us wash him. He was just kind of talking...chuckling as they do, 'heh, heh, heh'...picking up his feet and putting them down—just ever so slightly prancing."

"As far as we were concerned, he was being the perfect gentleman, but Carol walked over to him and said, 'Lark, cut it out.'"

"Instantly, he relaxed with all four feet on the ground!"

"Lark is one of the easiest horses we work with," declares Brenda. "Once he's sufficiently teased up, you just turn him towards the dummy and say, 'Okay, Lark,' and he hops up and breeds."

"When he's done, he's like, 'Okay, here's my job well done.' Then he walks back to the trailer, Carol takes him home, turns him out in the lot next to his two favorite bay mares, and he's quiet all the rest of the day!"

"You couldn't do that with most stallions. We certainly wouldn't take our other studs out of the breeding shed and turn them out in a lot just a fenceline away from another mare!"

Rugged Lark's uncanny understanding and restraint runs counter to all natural, compelling instincts making his self-control all the more remarkable.

"Testosterone runs very deep in stallions," agrees Chris Cox. "And when it comes to people being in the way, sometimes there's no mercy."

"Rugged Lark loves to breed a mare as much as any stallion. He'll nicker and carry on a little bit, but he understands there's a place for it and a time for it. He knows when he's in front of people, he doesn't do that. When it's business, it's business. That's what makes him unique. He knows his place—when to perform for breeding and when to perform in front of people. That's a big distinction for a stud...actually, a lot of people can't keep that straight!"

Mike Corrington was also struck by Rugged Lark's remarkably cooperative attitude when it came to the business of training. "Rugged Lark's a rare horse, there's not many like him," says Mike. "I've worked with a few of his [get]—only two or three. They were nice; mind-wise they were good."

"They were good at what they wanted to do and you have to allow them that. I wanted one of them to be a reinin' horse, but he wanted to be a pleasure horse. There again, you have to allow a horse to be what he wants to be...kinda like a child."

"Even if you're a professor at a college and your wife's a banker, your kid might want to be a bullrider...and he might be a great bullrider. It's the same with horses, you can't make them be something they don't want to be."

*Butch Campbell started many Lark babies for Carol. "In just two weeks they'd be walking, trotting, loping, guiding, and trying."*

©Courtesy of The Western Horseman

*For his exhibitions and clinics, Chis Cox always uses Rugged Stinger.*

"But that's another thing that was great about Rugged Lark—he was happy being whatever it was you wanted to do. That's the thing that's soooo unusual."

Acknowledging that genetics is Mother Nature's creative grab bag—a bag full of tricks or treats with constant surprises—Carol promotes intelligent and carefully considered breeding.

Mother Nature's chromosomal cauldron is a bit like a pot of gold—pure gold may sound valuable, but in order to be useful, it needs to be combined with other elements. The nature of pure gold is soft and supple, thus the purer the gold, the weaker the link.

The strongest, most practical and sought-after gold is found in the form of a combination of elements, an alloy. When its purity is bolstered by blended strength, gold's luster may be intensified since it can now stand up to the rigors of burnishing. Thus, in order to gain the strength, color and durability needed to create a valuable product, other elements must be added to pure gold. As an alloy pure gold's value

*Lynn Palm on My Royal Lark*

can then be enhanced by art; only then does gold become costly jewelry.

Just like mixing pure gold with pure gold, in-breeding or improper line-breeding creates inherently weak results, and overbreeding within a single breed will eventually ruin the genetic brew. Responsible breeding is imperative and owners must diligently protect against overbreeding on all levels.

There is a great deal to be said for the hybrid vigor achieved through outcrossing, as proven by the blending of attributes from Lark's Thoroughbred sire and Quarter Horse dam. The special traits of Really Rugged coupled with those of Alisa Lark created a unique amalgam of temperament, intelligence, conformation and movement in Rugged Lark that surpassed each parent's individual gifts.

Their plain, little bay colt grew up with love, was trained with trust, and earned respect and adulation as he progressed from World Champion to Superhorse to Olympic Ambassador, to superstar, to super sire producing super get.

As the announcer at the 1996 Thirtieth Anniversary of the All American Quarter Horse Congress proclaimed, "Rugged Lark is like a famous actor whose every movie is a box office blockbuster. Everything he does, he does well...and he does it all!"

And it seems he passes it all on to his babies. As Rugged Lark's foals began arriving, getting trained, maturing and competing it became evident that this successful Superhorse was also a successful sire.

"There's a lot of great horses, but there are not a lot of great horses that can produce," notes Chris Cox. "Rugged Lark is one that does produce and that makes him extra-special."

According to many, what Rugged Lark produces is also extra-special, as trainer Butch Campbell reports, "This horse has such an exceptional mind...he has so much mind to give his babies. They say that horses learn by repetition, but Lark takes very little repetition. You show him one thing one day and you never have to repeat it."

"And that's the way a lot of his babies are—you don't drill or go over and over.... The amazing thing about Lark's babies is what you can do with them in just two weeks. Carol would bring me a colt and after two weeks he'd have learned what it takes most colts anywhere from forty-five to sixty days to get. In just fourteen days, Rugged Lark's babies were already under saddle—walking, trotting, loping around, already guiding and trying. Occasionally there'd be one that took longer, but very rarely did I have to put more than thirty days on one of Lark's babies."

"Training his babies is good in one way and a hindrance in another way. Because they're so simple and quick, training his babies can make you feel you're well beyond the horse trainer that you are. They're so willing all the time, I'd just crack out his babies and that kinda makes you feel like you're a great trainer. You know...here you can do in two weeks what takes other horses so much longer."

"I rode so many Lark babies in a row that when I'd get a different colt in, I'd have to revamp and remember, 'Oops, this is not a Rugged Lark baby, we're going to have to go a little slower, we're going to do a little more repetition...'"

"He's passed on those traits very well," Butch concludes. "He's a very strong breeder in that way."

Veteran breeder and horse broker Blair Folck was equally impressed, "In 1988, Nancy and I stopped at Bo-Bett on the way down to our place in Florida and saw a crop of Rugged Lark colts barely broke to lead."

"Two months later, when we came back, they were riding those same colts through water, over bridges, picking up their leads and everything else. It was amazing how they're so darn smart—you don't have to teach them much, they just seem to know it."

Leslie Groves tells of another world-caliber competitor who was entranced by Rugged Lark's offspring: "One of my friends showed Look Who's Larkin' in the calf-roping at the World Show and got to take him down to his place for about six days to prepare him for the event. Now this fellow's been around a jillion horses in his life, but he was so taken with Look Who's Larkin's temperament, his physical ability, and mostly his willingness that he booked a mare to him."

After working with Rugged Lark, Chris Cox took home one of his sons. "Carol wanted me to have a Rugged Lark [colt] to take on his legacy. That's the reason I bought Rugged Stinger. He and I do demonstrations all over the United States and Canada. I start a lot of colts with him, and he's a big crowd pleaser on the road performing in clinics at Equitana, EquiWest, Calgary Stampede...."

"Having picked up a lot of good traits of his dad's, he's quite a horse himself—strong, but more 'quarter-horsey' than Rugged Lark. I do reining and cutting, I can rope off him and could probably compete in dressage with him. We do all those things...if I can think it, he'll react to it."

And of course, after sixteen years together, Lynn Palm Pittion-Rossillon is not only sold on the magic of Rugged Lark, she's continuing his legacy by owning and training his offspring.

"Rugged Lark's got it all as good as you'd want it to be," says Lynn. "I've got a son of his, My Royal Lark, that's a hunter-type out of a Thoroughbred mare. He's almost all that good, but there's little ounces here and there that aren't quite as strong as Rugged Lark."

"I've also got Rugged Painted Lark, the only paint stallion, and he's got some very special qualities, too. He's the Western type, so he'll be the reiner, the roper, that kind of a horse."

"Personally, I like the English-type Appendix Quarter Horse, because you can do all the Hunt-Seat events, and—depending on the horse again—you can also do Trail, Western Riding, Horsemanship, and Equitation. So there you've really got your Western and English horse—your all-around horse—while the Western-type horse can't do English. But that's the way the breed is going now."

"In the 1980's the all-around horse that did both English and Western was peaking. Today, national events are so specialized that most horses are bred and trained to compete either English or Western—not both, though you may still see some of the dual competition on the regional level."

"The Lark Ascending, in 1991, is the last Superhorse that did both English and Western events. So since '91, the Superhorse has been an English-only horse or a Western-only horse.

"But if ever there's a horse I've had that I think I could do another Superhorse with, it would be My Royal Lark. As an English-type horse, his best event will probably be the Working Hunter, but he's got Western ability, too. He's doing Trail and Western Riding very well."

"If I do the Superhorse again, on a horse that I've trained, I'd want to go back with both English and Western events, because what interests me is that this breed can do so many different things."

Each and every owner of a celebrated stallion prays that his horse will pass on its winning ways. But as Patty Shortino observes, success in competition does not necessarily guarantee success in breeding. "It's really rare that a great

(top left photo)
Longtime friends, Blair & Nancy Folck,
owners of many fine horses.

(top right photo) Lark congratulates his son, Heavy Duty Lark, on his Versatility Class win at the All American Quarter Horse Congress.

(bottom photo) Lieutenant Lark, AQHA GMC Truck Award winner, being driven by Lynn Palm.

(top photo) Regal Circle and Regal Lark, both by Rugged Lark, show off three World Championship trophies. Shane George rode them both.

(bottom photo) Rugged Dusty, 1994 AQHA World Champion in Heeling. Owned by Joan Hoyt and ridden by Robbie Schroeder.

show horse becomes a great sire. Usually great show horses will only sire another great one every now and then, but Rugged Lark's a rare individual in that regard...look what his get have done!"

Practically from the start of his breeding career, Rugged Lark has produced winners with his 1984 colt, Rugged Hour, becoming an AQHA Youth Champion and both his 1985 colt, Heavy Duty Lark, and his 1986 colt, Lieutenant Lark (the big-ball-loving youngster described in chapter nine), becoming AQHA Versatility Champions.

Here again, versatility is the operative word for the Rugged Lark line with impressive world champion results in both Western and Hunt Seat events:

Heza Lark Step, 1991 Junior Hunter Hack World Champion

Larks Lambata, 1994 World Champion Jr. Trail Horse

Regal Circle, 1994 World Champion Junior Hunter Hack and 1994 World Champion Green Working Hunter

Rugged Dusty, 1994 World Champion Junior Heeling

Rugged Bit O'Shiney, 1996 Youth World Champion Dally Team Roping-Heeling

Rugged Son, 1997 World Champion Hunter Hack

Larks Best Reason, 1999 AQHA Performance Champion, AQHA Superior All-Around and recipient of the AQHA Versatility Award

Its A Question Lark, 1999 Youth World Champion Reining

In addition to world championships, these and other Rugged Lark offspring have chalked up scores of superior and high-point titles and earned thousands of dollars in reining competition prize money with Berry Lark and Lark Bar Money both becoming NRHA World Champions.

Now Rugged Lark's talented offspring are out there competing and adding new chapters to the AQHA's history book:

In 1991 Rugged Lark became the first Superhorse to sire a Superhorse when his 1987 son, The Lark Ascending, won the prized title. That same year, The Lark Ascending also won World Champion Green Working Hunter and World Champion Junior Working Hunter honors, and in 1992, he returned to win the World Champion Senior Working Hunter title.

A year later, a 1989 Rugged Lark son, Regal Lark, became the 1993 Reserve World Show Superhorse—missing the top spot by only a single point. Regal Lark earned an impressive list of other awards as well, including the 1993 World Champion Green Working Hunter, Superior Hunter Under Saddle, Superior Green Working Hunter, High-Point Junior Working Hunter, High-Point Working Hunter Stallion, High-Point Junior Hunter Under Saddle, High-Point Hunter Under Saddle Stallion, High-Point Junior Hunter Hack, and High-Point Hunter Hack Stallion. In 1994, Regal Lark was the AQHA Performance Champion, the World Champion Senior Hunter Hack and Superior Working Hunter.

Another bit of history was made at Bo-Bett Farm in 1994 when Carol's two-time Superhorse was bred to the 1988 Superhorse, One For The Record, making their stud-colt, Lark's One For The Money, the first issue of two Superhorses. Three years later, One For The Record's owners, Bruce and Sue Kaplow, welcomed a nice filly, That's A Record, from the same Superhorse match.

Yet another notable breeding

*(top photo) Rugged Bit O'Shiney was a 5-time High Point Youth horse. He is pictured with proud owner, C.R. Bradley, after winning the Youth Calf Roping, Youth Team Heading and Youth Team Heeling at the 1995 All American Quarter Horse Congress.*

*(bottom photo) Lark's One For The Money, owned by Gary & Stacy Schaefer & ridden by Bill Ellis is currently winning at AHSA shows.*

(top photo) AQHA Versatility Champion, Lark's Best Reason

(bottom photo) Berry Lark is pictured after winning another Reining championship for trainer Rick Weaver.

triumph occurred in 1996 when Rugged Lark became the proud father of twins!

"At the time, we didn't know we were having twins," recalls Carol. "But the mare was huge...enormous! When she foaled someone asked, 'What is it—a colt or a filly?'"

"I said, 'It's got to be a filly because it's not big enough to be a colt.'"

"Wendy had gone back to the office to write down the time it had arrived. When she came back, we were watching the mare when, 'My God, here come some more feet'...and out came another one! We named them Fiddle and Faddle—Lark's Fiddle and Lark's Faddle."

Due to the physical stress they put on the mare, successful multiple births are rare in horses. Obviously, Bo-Bett's Thoroughbred mare, My Endora, was up to the challenge, for both youngsters are doing well. Not long ago, Carol presented Faddle to Chris Cox who plans to use him as a demonstration horse in his clinics, and Fiddle, still owned by Carol is being qualified for the World Show 2000 by Alfred Hewitt.

Incredibly, Rugged Lark's super legacy turned out yet another winner in 1999 when Larry Bryson's stallion, Look Who's Larkin', took the Superhorse title under Western tack in five difficult events.

Such an outstanding record for a stallion's progeny was not lost on USET Executive Director, Bob Standish, "Rugged Lark's exceptional to say the least, and certainly typifies what we aspire to achieve in our breeding program. To validate that end we've bred to Rugged Lark. We just sold a yearling filly by him and another mare's about to foal any day now."

"Obviously the fact that he achieved the Superhorse rating twice, plus sired two, and one reserve Superhorse shows that he puts an extraordinary athleticism into his foals.

He's made a lot of people want to own a Quarter Horse. I can think of no better validation of a horse's ability than to sire winning athletes."

By breeding up true with so many competitively super get, Rugged Lark has added yet another unprecedented success to his career—proving that in addition to being a Superhorse and a superstar, he's also a super sire.

As Don McDuffee notes, "It doesn't matter who you are, you have to respect this horse and what he's done for our industry...not only as an individual, but as a sire."

As Goodwill Ambassador on tour all over the country, Rugged Lark packs the stands.

He's won tremendous respect from everyone from the young child with the Breyer horse to the number one trainer or professional horseman of the year.

"He's the only horse to have won the Superhorse twice and produce two Superhorses: one in hunt seat and one in cow horse, reining and roping. No other horse has done that.

When an equine body, mind and spirit blend into one harmonious, willing entity the results are fantastic and rare. A trainer of hundreds of horses and man of few words, Mike Corrington spends a good part of every day in the saddle, but has yet to find another equal to Rugged Lark, "As far as I'm concerned, Rugged Lark's talent and temperament go beyond 'Super'. It's higher than that because there are a lot of talented or gifted horses, and if you work hard enough you're able to create something great with them...that becomes your Superhorse."

"But with Lark, you didn't have to work hard, you just had to spend a little time with him—not work, not effort, just time...now that's the ultimate horse!"

Others, such as auctioneer and horseman Blair Folck, ponder Lark's untapped potential, "I think the cattle events would be right down his alley because of his natural intelligence and all we'd have to have done was to have shown him and let him enjoy it. He would have taken care of cattle, I'm sure."

After Rugged Lark's appearance at an elaborate "Stop the Violence" fundraising benefit put on by

(top photo) Itsa Question Lark, owned by Alexa Warren, Youth World Champion Reining - 1998.
(bottom photo) The Lark Ascending and Marie Monda Zdunic win at the District 2 Fourth Level Freestyle (all breeds) Dressage.

*Lark Bar Money and Rocky Dare.
Another winning team for Rugged Lark.*

Abigail Wexner in Ohio, champion grand prix rider, Debbie Stephens told Carol she would have loved to have shown Lark in Grand-Prix Jumping.

Carol recalls, "She pointed to some huge jumps in the arena and said he could have been a big-time jumper. I said, 'Certainly not those kinds of fences!'"

"Now, this woman's at the top of her field, and she said, 'Why not?'"

Obviously, Rugged Lark's untried potential in stock events or Grand-Prix Jumping can only be imagined, but that potential may yet be realized in his get.

"Lark's nineteen years-old now and Carol's still calling me up to perform with him," Chris Cox marvels. "At the last few demonstrations we've done, she's made the comment that they were the best she's ever seen."

"All the people who took a part in training this horse...it was all very well done and Lynn Palm was certainly a big part of it. For me to be the last person on the ladder after what he's accomplished...and the horse still wants to learn to do more. It's such an honor for me that Carol thinks that I can help him do more."

"But you can't teach this horse what he does. Because of the grace that he has, riding Rugged Lark is...a very moving experience. He picks up on such subtle cues, he's so in-tune, just naturally together in his movements and mentality. I'd take him for rides out in the pasture and let him be a horse...it was

*(top left photo) Harold "Huddy" Hudspeth, everybody's friend.*

*(top right photo) Larks Fagan, owned by Bob Standish. "When you see Lark's babies, by golly, they carry his mark!"*

kind of a spiritual experience."

"We want all our horses to be smooth and graceful, and we want all our horses to be happy. For this horse to have done all he's done, with two Superhorse titles and now at nineteen to still be as happy as he is...that says a lot."

Still going strong at nineteen with a full complement of mares to breed, Rugged Lark is sowing a legacy that will survive him and grow in stature with his offspring.

"Over the years I've looked at a lot of horses, and the great ones that stand out in your mind become a benchmark," says Keith Bradley. "If anybody's got something that can compare to those, they've got themselves a fantastic individual."

"Rugged Lark's got a great head and a neat hip on him and when you see his babies, by golly they carry his mark! That's something I get a kick out of."

"And another fun thing about watching bloodlines...a lot of times part of the name will be in there so you can identify [ancestors].... Back in 1972 or '73 at one of my announcing jobs at the Congress, there were old cowboy judges like Harold Hudspeth from Oklahoma, and others, who came off ranches and knew horses from the ground up. They played a kind of genetic guessing-game, saying, 'I'll tell you that horse's bloodlines, then you tell me its name and we'll see if it fits.'"

"And they did! I'd sit there while they called off four or five stallions' offspring. I was just

*In 1999, Rugged Lark sired another Superhorse. His versatile son, "Look Who's Larkin", acquired the 1999 Superhorse title with points in Reining, Calf Roping, Working Cow Horse, and Heading and Heeling events. He was ridden by Doug Clark, Rick Rosashi and Todd Bergen for proud owners, Larry & Lynne Bryson.*

*1999 Superhorse, Look Who's Larkin'
celebrates his big win with friends and family.*

overwhelmed and asked, 'How can you do that?'"

"They said, 'You know your neighbor? Do his kids look like him?'"

"I said, 'Sure.'"

"'Well, there you are.' They said, 'You don't live around these things, and raise 'em and breed 'em without knowing one family from another.'"

"What a great awakening for me, listening to those guys."

"Now Rugged Lark himself will go down in history as an outstanding stallion and an outstanding performer, but another thing that's so great is that twenty, twenty-five, thirty years from now they'll be able to say 'That's an old Rugged Lark offspring, you can tell....'"

Carol is careful about breeding, but she's no elitist, so Rugged Lark's legacy is not reserved for the top echelons. She wants his offspring welcomed into all sorts of homes from Olympic heights to America's backyards and everything in between.

"He's such a dominant sire he can improve any mare," says Carol. "I've tried to keep his fees reasonable so that many can afford him and enjoy his babies as much as I have."

Unlike a lot of the top show- and racehorses, Lark's mellow temperament allows for most any competent horselover to be able to own, handle and enjoy one of his offspring.

*(top photo) Regal Lark, 1993 Reserve Superhorse, clears a fence on the way to his title.*

*(bottom right photo) Dorothy Randals, Carol Harris and Jimmie Randals at the Hall of Fame ceremony.*

*(bottom left photo) Lark's Smooth Move, "Smoothie", as a suckling.*

*Lark and Lynn Palm with (left to right): Kathleen Raine, Debbie Stephens, Karen O'Connor and David O'Connor.*

The AQHA's Bill Brewer is the proud owner of Lark's Smooth Move. When asked if "Smoothie" was a special horse for him Bill replied, "Sure he is...he's Smoothie. We have more fun with him! Everybody around here knows Smoothie—everybody. He's really special...."

"He's out of a mare called Just My Judy, whose mother, Judy Dell, was bred by one of my very close friends, Jimmie Randals. I admire and respect both Carol Harris and Jimmie Randals as horse people and as people. They were both AQHA judges and breeders who bred horses all their lives."

"I'm not a trainer and Smoothie can do a lot more than me—a lot more than me! He always goes with his ears forward and I love the way he moves out. He has one of the best walks that you'll ever see. The man that trained him also keeps him for me because I travel and I'm busy all the time. He rides him a lot more than I do and he's trained him to ride with an extended walk. Smoothie can walk faster than most horses jog."

"Being a little over sixteen hands, he is big...we liked him a lot better around fifteen-two when he was a three-year-old. As I've gotten older and he's gotten taller, life's gotten more complicated."

"But the thing that makes me proudest of him is when we go on rides to working ranches like the Bell Ranch or the Pitchfork Ranch and the cowboys—I'm talking about the real cowboys that ride—they always want to know about the big sorrel horse. That makes you feel really good."

Thankfully, with Rugged Lark's living legacy breeding up strong, many more horselovers will be able

Rugged 174 Lark

to feel really good enjoying life out on a Lark.

To be sure, Rugged Lark is extraordinary in many ways, yet at the same time, he's just a well-bred American Quarter Horse stallion who's had the benefit of love, trust, and perceptive training with—perhaps—just a touch of celestial guidance.

But as his signature song so aptly proclaims, Rugged Lark seized his moment in time and made it shine, becoming a winner for a lifetime by being the very best he could be. At first only one, he's no longer alone, and through his talented get he's becoming even more than anyone thought he would be. With his incredible record and powerful progeny the legend and legacy of America's Superhorse, Rugged Lark, will shine on...for eternity.

(opposite page)
*Lark's Smooth Move and owner, Bill Brewer, in his favorite place, Palo Duro Canyon, New Mexico.*

(top photo) Rugged Lark.
"Carol always loved horses with good heads and eyes that looked right through you."

(bottom photo) *Rugged Lark twins pictured at 20 & 35 minutes old in 1996. The colt on the right is Lark's Fiddle and on the left is Lark's Faddle.*

*The End*

*(opposite page)*
*Carol and Lark enjoy a quiet moment together.*

# Postscript

## Carol Has The Last Word

Many of us, in trying to reach perfection, are often destroying more than we accomplish. Most of the time we're not even aware of it. Sometimes when I'm working with my horses and dogs, I have a feeling that God is trying very hard to tell me something - to stop asking for "so much". Why not be satisfied with a little less, done a little easier and prettier? Is it the degree of difficulty that makes us believe that more is better? Our horses have no choices - they cannot say, "Hey there, this is too hard for me, can't you take it easy?" It is amazing to me what human athletes are being compelled to do today in order to be competitive. Humans can say yes or no but horses and animals are completely dependent on us to make choices for them. My fear is that since we tend to do everything so excessively, our judgement is way less than perfect. As an example: our Quarter Horses that are hunters must be very tall, not because they can jump better or make the strides between fences easier, but because they fit "the look". If they are 17 hands, they are supposed to look more like hunters and naturally, if they are thin, some think they are even better. All this is absurd and especially insulting to the intelligence of true horsemen. Our Western Pleasure horses today must be slow, excessively slow, and of course, they must fit the look. Why must they be so slow?

The cost of owning and showing horses has also become excessive. Hats, boots, clothes, saddles, bridles, trailers, trucks, entries, stalls, trainers, farriers, veterinarians, and of course, horses, may send us all to the poor house. Where will it end and who is able to end it? Leadership is a possibility but first our leaders must recognize that we have a problem–I feel our judges could easily become our leaders and our trainers could easily start developing the kind of horse that just plain normal people enjoy.

Rugged Lark was, and still is, such a horse. He is not excessively anything. He is merely an animal that did everything he was asked to do well. I always tried to give him trainers that respected him, that could help him perform his God-given talents in a way that would protect his mind. Lark was not unbeatable, but he was constantly a winner mostly because he was permitted to enjoy his work. His health, his attitude and his beauty, at age 19, have not changed.

Everything Lark did was affordable. Expenses were as carefully watched as he was. No glitz, just functional good care. Even when the public was in awe of him, they could still touch and relate to him.

I feel that there is a breaking point when too much pizazz might tend to discourage newcomers from enjoying our sport. They might fear they cannot compete on such an expensive level. I know it could easily have stopped me cold had I started in horses today, however I absolutely feel that the opportunity to enjoy this sport and be a winner still exists for the horse lover who doesn't have "big bucks". Anyone who has an eye, a mind, a little patience, and the ability to listen to sound advice can still excel in this business. All the expensive toys that we now surround ourselves with are not really necessary and have very little to do with competition or breeding. Regarding our youth–why can't they still compete in a clean pair of jeans, a starched white shirt, polished boots and a neatly creased hat? I would love to see the young girls look like little kids again instead of Jon-Benet look-a-likes. I know it's fun to show off our kids, but why so excessively?

I've enjoyed becoming an "ancient senior citizen" because I no longer hesitate to say what I think. I'm still hoping that people won't get totally upset, but I just want so badly for certain things in our industry to be practical and remain accessible to everyone.

My heart belongs to the American Quarter Horse and all the fine people who every day are enforcing our rules, keeping our records and smoothly running our business. Along with Lark, I feel these folks are a special part of my family, but I realize they are not able to set the standards by which we judge our horses and each other. We, the membership, must take on this responsibility and we must try hard to show our association that we can do just as good a job as they do. If we can make this happen, there is no doubt in my mind that the American Quarter Horse will remain forever the most respected symbol of equine perfection in the entire world. I'm proud to have been a part of it.

*Carol*

*Darcy Clark, daughter of Doug Clark on*

*'Look Who's Larkin' in November, 1999.*

**BO-BETT FARM**
MATERNITY WARD
VISITING HOURS 9AM-4PM
*Specializing in the Get of Rugged Lark*
ALL OUR FOALS GET A SUPER HORSE START!

Here Lies The Last S.O.B. Who Stole My Feed

OLD DOGS
YOUNG DOGS
SEVERAL - STUPID DOGS
PLEASE DRIVE SLOWLY

**BO-BETT FARM**
SINCE 1964
MATERNITY WARD
ALL FOALS RECEIVE SPECIAL ATTENTION BY
*Carol, Wendy And The Staff*
ATTENDING VET - DR. LARRY SHAFFER

All photos on this page ©Reg Corkum

We in Florida are proud to claim Rugged Lark as a Florida-Bred Champion! Carol, you and Lark have been great ambassadors for the Florida horse industry. We are very grateful and appreciative.

Richard E. Hancock
Executive Vice President, FTBOA

*"Every day I worry about my foals, my mares,*

*those stupid dogs, and somebody stealin' my feed -*

*I don't even dare close my door to get some rest!"*

Patsy Geier on Pars Rugged Lark

Larks Alibi and Alfred Hewitt

Suzanne Miller and Maggie Starlark

Dick Morgan and Phantom Lark

**Cool Hand Lark with Shawn Flarida**

**Larks First Step and Shawn Flarida**

"Heart, You've gotta have Heart," I guess is a good way to sum up both Carol and Lark, a lady with a huge compassionate heart and an animal with all the try in the world. That's why they've made such a team. I'm lucky to know them both."
David Conners ❀ Trainer

**Sheza Rugged Lark and Clark Bradley**

**Meadow Lark Lime and Sam Ely**

*Our Gallant Lark*

*Larks Hanky Panky*

*Rugged Hour*

&

*Samantha Hess*

*The Twins*
*Larks Faddle & Larks Fiddle*

©D.J. Fitzgerald

*My Royal Lark*

# Author's Note

I am most grateful to Carol Harris for the time, trust, knowledge and laughs we shared throughout this project. It has been a true privilege getting to know her and Rugged Lark.

Thanks also to Carol's many friends and associates who so generously gave of their time and memories.

A special thanks to everyone at Bo-Bett—especially Barbara who kept us on track and organized throughout.

# Carol's Note

A special thank you to Barbara Feehrmeyer for her editing assistance. – To Barbara Hooker, my loyal secretary, for her constant support. – And to Tom and Amy Grabe of Endeavor Publications, Inc. for their understanding and guidance.

Carol, I can remember a rather funny situation that happened in 1975. You, I, Dr. Barry Wood and Clyde Kennedy judged the AJQHA World in Tulsa, Oklahoma. We had just arrived at the hotel one night after judging all day. We were all walking through the lobby of the hotel and for some reason we stopped at the registration desk. One of the girls working behind the desk had a very full and fluffy hair-do. Being the nice person that you are, you told her how much you adored her hair. Clyde Kennedy spoke up and said, "Carol, why are you lying to that girl? You told us that you thought she looked like an angora goat." You thought really quickly and smoothed it over with the girl. Then, we all started to our rooms. You went ahead of the three of us and hid around the corner of the hallway. As Clyde came around the corner, you hit him over the head with your hairbrush. It made a very loud noise as he had a steel plate in the top of his head. At that point, you were really afraid that you had injured him. He was ok.

Billy Steel - AQHA Director of Judges

Great Horse! Great Lady! She has the whole picture in perspective, whether it's horses or people. Her attitude about life is contagious. It is an honor to be her friend, and being her neighbors becomes a unique bonus.

Tim & Lou Petty, Breeder & Owners

I had the pleasure of seeing Lark work his "magic" on many occasions, every time to standing ovations and with tears in my eyes. Carol - there will never be another like "you two".

Everett Salley, AQHA Past President

CAROL, WE CONSIDER OURSELVES BLESSED IF WE HAVE ONE GREAT HORSE TO RIDE IN A LIFETIME. YOU ARE FORTUNATE TO HAVE HAD SEVERAL, BUT LARK IS SPECIAL. HE WAS INTENDED TO BE YOUR FRIEND AND I BELIEVE GOD PLANNED IT THAT WAY.

SARAH BRADLEY, TRAINER & JUDGE

God created the heaven and earth and he also created Carol Harris and Rugged Lark. He is still trying to figure out which are his greatest accomplishments. Certainly Carol and Lark will go down in the history of the AQHA as two of our greatest Ambassadors. I feel very privileged to have known them both.

Jack Anderson, AQHA Past President

Carol & Lark - A super duo! Our first big outing with Carol and Lark was at the World Cup. The AHSA was impressed with Lark in his tux, drinking champagne out of a silver bowl. Our chalet reception tent had the largest attendance. They've never disappointed us!

Jim Barton, AQHA Past President

Carol,
We loved your picture on the front of the journal and the article, also. We love you and are proud you are a friend of the Virginia Quarter Horse Association.

Mary & Steve Shivers

---

Dear Carol,
What a wonderful visit at Bo-Bett again this year, from having Rugged Lark greet us in the office to having the bald eagle appear on command. Thanks so much for allowing my class to keep returning to your farm. We've been doing this since 1972.

Sincerely,
Anthony Borton
Professor, University of Massachusetts

---

Dear Mrs. Harris,
Thank you for allowing the University of Georgia horse judging team to visit Bo-Bett Farm. We especially appreciated you taking the time to share your knowledge and expertise and the students enjoyed getting to know Rugged Lark. The team dominated the contest. This success is because of the workout we had at your farm.

Sincerely,
Patrick Kayser
Equine Educational Specialist

---

Dear Carol & Rugged Lark,
Thank you so much for the pictures and model you sended us. Rugged Lark is the prettiest horse I have ever seen.
Love,
Jaclyn Wilson

PS - My sister Hannah can't write but she sends her love too.

---

Carol and Rugged Lark have been Good Will Ambassadors for the American Quarter Horse. Lark combines tremendous athletic ability with a kind, gentle human-like disposition. He has reached out and touched the hearts of horse lovers everywhere.

Jerry & Patti Robertson
Breeders & Trainers

---

Dear Lark,
i am your biggest, smallest fan. i am sending you my picture.

brandy barnell, age 5

# Disclaimer

Since the author worked directly from tapes, at times it was necessary to modify spoken phrasing to wording more conducive to written text. In doing so, care was taken to preserve content, however quotes were no longer strictly verbatim. All conversations have been reported as closely to the original transcript as possible. The author apologizes if any oversights, misquotes, mistakes, misunderstandings, or errors occur in the text as they are completely unintentional.

The opinions expressed in this book were given freely and are those of the individual contributors or the author, not necessarily of the publisher. The author attempted to reference and verify all pertinent information, however, due to the very nature of conversational anecdotes, total verification is not possible.

Most photographs are from the personal collection of Carol Harris and Bo-Bett Farm. A sincere attempt was made to contact photographers, identify subjects and to give appropriate credit. However, due to the lapse of time or incomplete documentation, it was not possible to reach all involved and we regret if proper permission or credit was inadvertently omitted.

# Photographic Acknowledgements

**Prelude**
| | |
|---|---|
| Cappy Jackson | iv |
| D.J. Fitzgerald | vi |
| D.J. Fitzgerald | viii |
| Cappy Jackson | xi |
| Courtesy of AQHA | xii |

**Chapter 1**
| | |
|---|---|
| Bob Judy | facing page 1 |
| Jim Jernigan | 1 |
| Courtesy of Bo-Bett | 1 |
| Pompano Park Raceway | 2 |
| Pompano Park Raceway | 3 |
| Jim Jernigan | 4 |
| T. Becker & NRHA | 4 |
| Harold Campton | 5 |
| Harold Campton | 6 |
| Doug Leahy | 6 |
| Dalco | 7 |
| Courtesy of Bo-Bett | 7 |
| Harold Campton | 8 |
| Haggin | 9 |
| Doug Leahy | 11 |
| Courtesy of Bo-Bett | 12 |

**Chapter 2**
| | |
|---|---|
| Bob Judy | 15 |
| Barbara Jean Strickland | 16 |
| Courtesy of Bo-Bett | 17-19 |

**Chapter 3**
| | |
|---|---|
| D. J. Fitzgerald | 22 |
| Courtesy of Bo-Bett | 23 |
| Sarah Gentry | 24 |
| Reg Corkum | 25 |
| D. J. Fitzgerald | 26 |
| Courtesy of Ron & Jay Nanfelt | 27 |
| Doug Leahy | 27 |
| Sarah Gentry | 28 |
| Kerry Heubeck | 28 |
| Doug Leahy | 29-30 |

**Chapter 4**
| | |
|---|---|
| Mary Phelps | 34 |
| Harold Campton | 35-36 |
| Courtesy of Bo-Bett | 37-38 |
| Harold Campton | 39 |

**Chapter 5**
| | |
|---|---|
| Sarah Gentry | 42 |
| Reg Corkum | 43 |
| Courtesy of Isabel Robson | 43 |
| Ashbey-Tatham | 44 |
| Sarah Gentry | 44-45 |
| D. J. Fitzgerald | 45 |
| Sarah Gentry | 46 |
| Reg Corkum | 47 |
| D. J. Fitzgerald | 47 |
| Courtesy of Bo-Bett | 47 |
| Cappy Jackson | 48-49 |
| Courtesy of Bo-Bett | 49 |
| TAG Photographics | 50 |
| Reg Corkum | 52 |
| Sarah Gentry | 50 |

**Chapter 6**
| | |
|---|---|
| Endeavor Graphics | 54 |
| Harold Campton | 55 |
| Courtesy of Lynn Palm | 56 |
| Courtesy of Patty Shortino | 59 |
| Dashing | 60 |
| Harold Campton | 61 |
| Sandy Lee | 62 |
| Harold Campton | 63-66 |
| Grace "E" | 67 |
| Harold Campton | 67-68 |
| Courtesy of Bill & Ann Lanning | 68 |
| Courtesy of Bo-Bett | 69-70 |
| Harold Campton | 71-73 |

**Chapter 7**
| | |
|---|---|
| Harold Campton | 76-77 |
| Cappy Jackson | 79 |
| Courtesy of Dr. Marvin Beeman | 79 |
| Breyer Mfg. | 81 |
| Harold Campton | 83 |
| John C. Totton | 84 |
| Harold Campton | 84 |
| Courtesy of The Quarter Horse Jnl. | 85 |
| Frank Flynn | 85 |

**Photo Pages (no numbers)**
| |
|---|
| Reg Corkum |
| Reg Corkum |
| Courtesy of Bo-Bett |
| Reg Corkum |
| Courtesy of Bo-Bett |
| Hank Cohen |
| D. J. Fitzgerald |
| Scott Banghart |
| D. J. Fitzgerald |
| Courtesy of Bo-Bett |
| Jim Jernigan |

**Chapter 8**
| | |
|---|---|
| Mary Phelps | 88 |
| Judith Berk | 91 |
| Bob Tarr | 93 |
| Courtesy of AQHA | 93 |
| Courtesy of AQHA | 94 |
| Courtesy of Bo-Bett | 95 |
| D. J. Fitzgerald | 96 |
| Courtesy of AQHA | 97 |
| Courtesy of Bo-Bett | 97 |
| Cheryl Binder | 98 |
| Reg Corkum | 99 |
| Leslie Sowder-Baker | 99 |
| Courtesy of Bo-Bett | 100-101 |
| Liz Goff | 102 |
| Ctsy. of The Philadelphia Inquirer | 103 |
| Courtesy of Bo-Bett | 103-107 |
| D.J. Fitzgerald | 107 |

**Chapter 9**
| | |
|---|---|
| D. J. Fitzgerald | 108 |
| Al Cook | 109 |
| Cappy Jackson | 110 |
| Sarah Gentry | 110 |
| Rebekah Witter | 111 |
| D. J. Fitzgerald | 111 |
| Harold Campton | 112 |
| Courtesy of Bo-Bett | 112-113 |
| Courtesy of The Quarter Horse Jnl. | 113 |
| Scott Banghart | 114 |
| June Mastracola | 114 |
| Endeavor Graphics | 114 |
| Sarah Gentry | 114 |
| Brent Walters | 114 |
| D. J. Fitzgerald | 115 |
| Sarah Gentry | 116-121, 124-129 |
| D. J. Fitzgerald | 130 |
| Sarah Gentry | 131 |
| Cynthia McFarland | 133 |

**Chapter 10**
| | |
|---|---|
| Sarah Gentry | 134 |
| Courtesy of Bo-Bett | 135-136 |
| Sarah Gentry | 136 |
| Courtesy of Bo-Bett | 136-137 |
| Sarah Gentry | 138-140 |
| Courtesy of Bo-Bett | 141 |
| Courtesy of Marilyn LaGrange | 142 |
| Courtesy of The Quarter Horse Jnl. | 143 |
| Harold Campton | 143 |
| Courtesy of Bo-Bett | 144 |
| Sarah Gentry | 144 |
| Mike Rastelli | 145 |
| Cynthia McFarland | 146 |
| Sarah Gentry | 147 |
| Tina Hines | 147 |
| Courtesy of Bo-Bett | 148-152 |
| Bruce Ackerman | 153 |

**Chapter 11**
| | |
|---|---|
| Carol Roark | 154 |
| Courtesy of The Quarter Horse Jnl. | 155 |
| Harold Campton | 156 |
| Reg Corkum | 157 |
| Waltenberry | 158 |
| Courtesy of Western Horseman | 159 |
| Cynthia McFarland | 160 |
| Larry Williams | 161 |
| Courtesy of Bo-Bett | 163 |
| Harold Campton | 163-164 |
| Dalco | 164 |
| Harold Campton | 165 |
| Sporting Images Photography | 165 |
| Cindy Coker | 166 |
| Waltenberry | 166 |
| Don Trout | 167 |
| Susan Sexton | 167 |
| Waltenberry | 168 |
| Chrisy Crouch | 169 |
| Courtesy of Bo-Bett | 169 |
| Cappy Jackson | 170 |
| K.C. Montgomery | 170-171 |
| Harold Campton | 172 |
| Courtesy of Bo-Bett | 172 |
| Harold Campton | 173 |
| Sarah Gentry | 175 |
| Courtesy of Bo-Bett | 175 |
| D.J. Fitzgerald | 176-177 |

**Conclusion**
| | |
|---|---|
| D.J. Fitzgerald | 178 |
| Reg Corkum | 182 |
| Reg Corkum | 183 |
| Harold Campton | 184 |
| P & J Production | 184 |
| Harold Campton | 184 |
| Waltenberry | 185 |
| Harold Campton | 185 |
| Jim Lee | 186 |
| D. J. Fitzgerald | 186 |
| Courtesy of Bo-Bett | 186 |
| Sarah Gentry | 186 |

**Cover Wrap**
| | |
|---|---|
| D.J. Fitzgerald | Front Cover |
| Leslie Groves | Back Cover |
| Rebekah F. Witter | Back Inside Wrap |

# A Poem For Lark

The first time I saw him,
With his kind and gentle eyes,
He quickly stole my heart,
But to me that's no surprise.

I've watched him through the years,
Rising up in all his glory,
But I can tell you now,
We'll not forget his story.

He's tall and dark and handsome,
With a heart so very true,
You'll quickly fall in love with him,
There's nothing you can do.

The last time I watched him move,
With beauty and with grace,
I couldn't help the tears that slid,
And dribbled down my face.

As I watched him take that final bow,
That very sad last night,
I came to realize this horse,
Will never lose the spotlight.

For glory, legends, fame and fans,
He'll always have a spark,
Because we never will forget,
The stallion - Rugged Lark.

Christy Hightower, one of Lark's young fans